HOW GREEN WAS MY VALLEY

THE SCREENPLAY FOR THE DARRYL F. ZANUCK FILM PRODUCTION DIRECTED BY JOHN FORD

PHILIP DUNNE

BASED ON THE NOVEL BY RICHARD LLEWELLYN

INTRODUCTORY ESSAY BY PHILIP DUNNE

SANTA BARBARA   •   SANTA TERESA PRESS   •   1990

FIRST EDITION
Limited to 1000 Hardbound Trade Copies
Plus 250 Special Copies Signed by
Philip Dunne and Roddy McDowall

ISBN 0-944166-04-0 TRADE EDITION
ISBN 0-944166-05-9 SPECIAL EDITION

LC 90-062189

PR
6023
.L47
H6
1990

MANUFACTURED IN THE UNITED STATES OF AMERICA

79 437
D92 K

for RODDY McDOWALL
who brought it to life

ACKNOWLEDGEMENTS

Books like films are collaborations with debts often owed to many. James Curtis, more than anyone else, encouraged us in our project, provided research, and much valued counsel. Rudy Behlmer kindly shared memos written by Darryl F. Zanuck to John Ford during the production of the film. Ned Comstock, Archives Assistant at the University of Southern California Cinema-Television Library and Archives of the Performing Arts, provided much background information, memos, and drafts of scripts for our reading. He went to great personal effort to aid our work. Brigitte J. Kueppers, Head of the Theater Arts Library at the University of California at Los Angeles, allowed us to view drafts of the screenplay and memos in their important collections. There is a dissertation on the evolution of the screenplay waiting to be written between the collections at USC and UCLA. The Manuscripts Department of the Lilly Library at Indiana University provided information from the John Ford Papers. The staff of the Margaret Herrick Library of the Academy of Motion Pictures Arts & Sciences were helpful. Malcolm Willits and Mark Willoughby helped with the extensive resources of their Collectors Bookstore in Hollywood.

Roddy McDowall has been gracious, helpful, and very giving of his time. Anna Lee kindly provided useful information. Alfred and Abra Shapiro were very supportive. Danny Burk of Burk Communications, Inc., of South Bend, Indiana shared rare John Ford films in his outstanding collection of motion pictures. Others to be thanked are Amanda Dunne, Deborah Sanford, Debra Reed, Dr. Jana Saunders, Dr. Paul Frizler, Peter & Lorraine Stern, Keith Croft, and Sasha Newborn.

James Pepper

No Fence Around Time

Philip Dunne

No Fence Around Time

I. Genesis

Where does a movie begin? At what precise point can we discern its newly fertilized egg, its Big Bang, its Genesis? The critic of *Time* magazine thought he knew how and when *How Green Was My Valley* came into being. "Director John Ford," he wrote in his unsigned 1941 review, "has chosen the book's method to tell his story: his reminiscing Welshman is an offscreen voice, introducing and commenting on the picture's episodes." Except for the cast, nobody else connected with the production is mentioned in his 700-word review.

Since the critic admits that in the Beginning was a Word, Richard Llewellyn's novel, this is not pure Auteur Theory, which holds that the movie springs full-armed—like Pallas Athena from the brow of Zeus—out of the cerebrum of its director, but it will take nothing away from my cherished friend Jack Ford's brilliant direction and his well-deserved Academy Award to say that the review, like so many others, gives a completely false impression of the movie's conception.

Then can we pinpoint the fertilization of the egg some time before that, when producer Darryl F. Zanuck and I had our first conference, and incidentally decided to tell "our" story in the book's reminiscent flashback? (We called the technique "narratage." I had been impressed by it when Preston Sturges and I were both working for Jesse Lasky at the old Fox Studio in 1933, and Preston used it in his innovative *The Power and the Glory*. It was also used in Sacha Guitry's 1936 *Le Roman d'un Tricheur* and over Stanley's march in our *Stanley and Livingstone* in 1939).

But it wasn't producer Zanuck's story, or mine. It was Richard Llewellyn's story, and the movie in truth was born when he sat down to write: "I am going to pack my two shirts with my other socks and my best suit in the little blue cloth my mother used to tie around her hair when she did the house, and I am going from the Valley." Those words, with which he opened his novel, slightly modified in my screenplay and spoken by narrator Irving Pichel over shots of the ruined valley, also opened the finished movie.

But there may have been an even earlier beginning. In 1961, when I was directing a picture in Wales, I was told that Llewellyn's haunting novel had been inspired by the diary of his father, who was himself perhaps the prototype of the novel's Huw Morgan. I had met Llewellyn in London, and always intended to ask about this, but never saw him again.

However he came by the idea, *How Green Was My Valley* began not with any individual or group at Twentieth Century-Fox, but with the descendant of Welsh coal miners who wrote it.

The movie made from his book, on the other hand, was the product of many minds, of many creative and technical skills. In sequence there were Hollywood's ablest producer of the period, not one but two world-famous directors, a glittering cast of actors, and the cameraman, composer, art director, film editor and all the other talented artists and technicians who made major contributions to the finished picture. Like all movies, it was, Auteur theorist critics to the contrary notwithstanding, an intricate and elaborate collaboration.

Parenthetically, I don't want to give the impression that I am prejudiced against critics, even though as both writer and director I have often been the target for their slings and arrows. Bosley Crowther of the *New York Times,* for instance, called *How Green Was My Valley* a "stunning pictorial masterpiece," but the only adjective he could find for my screenplay was "inadequate." He was certainly right on the first count, and possibly on the second as well. The screenplay followed the book in being quite frankly episodic; there was no other way to dramatize Llewellyn's many interwoven stories, stretched out over many years.

No, I don't dislike critics, but I detest some of the things they do. For instance, in analyzing a movie, some of them seem to feel compelled to sort out sheep from goats, to assign credit here and dish out blame there, whereas the truth is that in our collaborative art it is nearly always impossible, even for the actual participants, to decide which of us did or failed to do what. More often than not, the sacrificial goat turns out to be the writer.

For instance, my esteemed colleague, the late Mary McCall, Jr. (whose daughter happens to be a highly respected critic), wrote the *Maisie* series at MGM starring Ann Sothern. Mary used to carry in her purse a review by a prominent critic which mercilessly panned one of her screenplays, adding that the picture was saved only by the witty things Ann Sothern said.

When I was directing a movie at Universal, a veteran writer used to drop by my set to air his miseries. His latest script had fallen into the clutches of a darling of the critics, a young director who had skyrocketed to fame because of a competent job he had done in turning a hit play into a successful movie. Although he had merely photographed the play more or less intact, one critic, a dedicated Auteur theorist, had compared him to Fellini, Truffaut and Wyler, if not Jesus Christ. According to my friend, the director had taken his press notices to heart and begun to consider himself an author. Apparently, he and the star of the picture, who also harbored literary aspirations, were disemboweling his script on the set and turning it into a Grade B soap opera.

The picture opened to unanimously bad notices, but the worshipful critic rose to the challenge by telling his readers that this time the brilliant young director had been betrayed by "his" writer. Auteurs, it appears, are responsible for their hits, but not for their flops.

Strangely enough, my friend the writer was less incensed by being blamed for the movie's failure than by that little possessive pronoun. "Good, bad or indifferent," he growled, "I'm my own goddam writer."

In our collaborative craft, it is almost impossible to tell who provides the quantum jump which guarantees a movie's success. Julien Josephson and I share credit for writing *Stanley and Livingstone.* We had been asked to rewrite a very bad script and had no idea what to do with it when someone at the studio—

I have been told that it was executive William Drake—sent Zanuck a brief memo which completely transformed the story. On *Luck of the Irish*, the director, Henry Koster, was the hero. We were ready to go into production with what was, to me at least, a dubious script, when he made the saving suggestion. We were able to talk a somewhat reluctant Zanuck into delaying production for several weeks while I rewrote the script.

Sometimes one little scene, one piece of business, will turn a routine movie into an event in cinema history: James Cagney shoving half a grapefruit into Mae Clarke's face in *Public Enemy;* Richard Widmark pushing an old lady in a wheelchair down the stairs in *Kiss of Death;* the people who live near a railroad track having to interrupt conversation every time a train shakes their house on its foundation in *A Letter to Three Wives.* (As a matter of fact, I may have given writer-director Joe Mankiewicz the idea for that. During my government service during World War II, my wife and I lived in a tiny apartment some thirty feet removed from New York's Third Avenue elevated tracks. When trains rumbled past, our sometimes distinguished guests—James Thurber, John Hersey, John Ford—were forced into suspended animation.)

Certainly Jack Ford put his mark on *How Green Was My Valley.* His prints are all over it, it is shot in his inimitable style, and he contributed at least one of the touches that made the picture memorable: in the final sequence having Huw sing his father's name as he searches for him in the flooded mine. But to call it "his" picture to the exclusion of everyone else, as *Time*'s critic did, is to do a grave injustice to all the other contributors, in particular to Darryl Zanuck, who staked his reputation and perhaps his professional future on the picture's value, when all others had lost faith in it.

To gain full understanding of how the movie was made, and in particular how two justly famous directors came to be involved in it, we have to recreate in our minds the great film factories of mid-century, in particular what was often referred to as "the writers' studio," Darryl Zanuck's Twentieth Century-Fox.

II. Assembly Line

In these days when Hollywood studios are run by lawyers and accountants, with the actual movie-makers in effect camping on the premises only during the period of actual production, it is hard to project the imagination back fifty years and visualize a sort of film factory which turned out thirty or forty movies a year, with the movie-makers mostly on long-term contracts, working under the supervision of an iron-willed boss. Even more difficult is the notion of a virtual assembly line, with writers writing, directors directing, cutters cutting, with the director discouraged from participating in the writing process, the writer from visiting the set, both of them from the final editing stage, and one individual the sole and final arbiter at every stage of production.

Yet that is how the boy from Wahoo, Nebraska, Darryl F. Zanuck, ran his creation, Twentieth Century-Fox. I can best describe it as a strict but benevolent imperium, with Zanuck, no Caligula or Nero, its all-powerful Augustus.

It would be a perfectly legitimate question to ask how a system which deprived the writer of participating in the realization (as the French say) of his or her own script could be described as "the writers' studio." Nunnally Johnson, perhaps the most respected of all screenwriters (and an excellent director in his own right) supplied the best answer when he wrote that at Twentieth for a director to tamper with a script once approved by Zanuck was to insult American womanhood and trample on the flag. I had this forcibly brought home to me when I took to directing and changed a line of dialogue in my own script. Darryl came down on me like a ton of bricks. "Goddamit," he said, "for twenty years I've been protecting you from other directors, and now you force me to protect you from yourself." (I had made the change at the request of the star. When he next approached me with a "Phil, I've been thinking," I said quickly to my assistant, "Put this man in for a stunt check." If actors would like to live dangerously, let them take up wing-walking or window-washing, but nothing so perilous as rewriting dialogue.)

Nunnally has also been quoted as saying that the principal function of a director is to keep the actors from going home before six, but later amended this to explain that he was thinking of one particular director. But he did write of the director as seen by Auteur theorists: "He has all the qualities necessary for cultism . . . his powers are ghostly and not subject to worldly analysis, and his magic is visible only to his initiates. Religions have been started on far less."

He also wrote that Zanuck looked on directors as "glorified mechanics." I never heard Darryl say anything like that, but he did tell me that as long as he had a good script he didn't care much who directed it, though there were a few butchers he would rule out. Even that I can't accept as accurately reflecting his views. His attitude towards directors was much more ambivalent. He afforded them every courtesy, though there were a few notorious tyrants on the set he would lash with the tongue of an angry Marine drill sergeant in his office. Like all born executives, he was a keen judge of character, and knew that bullies usually can be bullied, nor was he averse to pushing over those intended by nature to be pushovers.

In "the writers' studio," director credits in advertising and publicity matched in prominence his own as producer, while, before the Screen Writers Guild at last won a correction, a magnifying glass was needed to discern the name of the writer.

Darryl's problem, I think, was that to some extent he swallowed the myth (as I did) that directors were endowed with some of Nunnally Johnson's ghostly powers. Directing was something he had never tried, and possibly feared he couldn't bring off.

Then, his imperium was the entire lot with all its multiple departments, but every director enjoyed, within this imperium, a little satrapy of his own. On the set, the director is an absolute monarch, though sometimes a ranking star can put a dent in his crown. Even the cans which rush the exposed film to the laboratories are stencilled with his name.

Orson Welles called a movie set the biggest electric train a boy ever had to play with—and so it is. I can never forget the feeling of walking on to a set for the first time as director, and facing several hundred men and women waiting for me to tell them what to do. It was both frightening and exhilarating, like my first solo in a plane. It was a taste of Power.

14

No wonder that a director begins to think of himself as the prime creator of the movie, and no wonder that an Auteurist critic, visiting the set and never meeting writer or producer, might become dazzled by the aura of power that surrounds the director. Even those little possessive pronouns play a part. My friend who objected to being called "his" writer, meaning the director's writer, was angry because the pronoun implied subordination, but the first time a lovely star introduced me to a set visitor as "our director," I inflated like Aesop's frog.

Darryl had no established place on the set, no function to perform, no chair with his name on it. He was in effect merely the guest of the director, just another tourist tripping over cables and getting in the way of busy professionals. And that, I believe, is why he rarely visited live sets (and why I as a writer preferred to avoid them). His command post was that long, long office, painted "Zanuck Green" and adorned with trophies of African hunts, or his luxurious projection room directly below it. There the minor satraps, the directors, had to come to him.

In spite of his remark implying that he considered the director relatively unimportant, Darryl cast his directors with the greatest of care. On *The Rains Came,* he decided that no suitable candidate was available on the lot, though several leading contract directors were itching for the assignment, and borrowed Clarence Brown from Metro-Goldwyn-Mayer. He told me that he wanted Clarence, Garbo's principal director, to help Myrna Loy (also borrowed from Metro) make the abrupt transition from All-American girls such as her Nora Charles in *The Thin Man* to our decadent and promiscuous Lady Esketh. Not that she needed any help; she took to the naughty lady like a duck to water. Such switches were nothing new to Myrna, a superb actress, born in Helena, Montana, who had served her Hollywood apprenticeship typecast as a sultry Eurasian.

On *How Green Was My Valley,* Darryl's first choice was also off the lot: he borrowed the rising directorial star William Wyler from Sam Goldwyn. And that is how not one but two world-famous directors, Wyler and Ford, came to participate in the production.

Wyler's contribution, though significant, was limited to the pre-production phase: casting, building of sets and, most important, to the final screenplay. He was the beneficiary of a waiver, granted to a few favored individuals, from Zanuck's policy of excluding directors from the writing phase. Like the creatures in Orwell's *Animal Farm,* some directors were more equal than others. Of those I worked with, Clarence Brown, Henry King and Ford himself were the other principal beneficiaries of the waiver.

But even where the favored few were concerned, the writing process was assumed to be complete before they were assigned. They were allowed to suggest changes, not to make them. Writers at Twentieth never wrote "for" directors, as most critics and movie historians assume; they wrote for Darryl Zanuck. Of the twenty-odd directors who shot screenplays which I wrote alone or in collaboration, I sat in story conferences with only a handful, and three I never even met (nor will I, since they have long since ascended to that big Sound Stage in the sky). In fact, the pictures they directed I have never seen, since I thoroughly disliked the assignments. In my early assembly line days I did what I was told to do, and only in later years did I earn the privilege of turning down assignments.

15

I should emphasize that in my opinion the Zanuck way was not the best way to make movies, though it's hard to quarrel with his track record. In the twenty years that he reigned supreme over Twentieth Century-Fox, "the writers' studio" won five Academy Awards for directors, one-fourth of the total awarded, and this against the competition of six other major studios, not to mention such formidable independents as Samuel Goldwyn and David O. Selznick. It worked for Zanuck—and failed miserably when he was succeeded by incompetents. It was then that what we never realized was a Golden Age came to an abrupt end.

At a February 1981 dinner at the University of Southern California's Town and Gown Society posthumously honoring Darryl Zanuck which I chaired, Roddy McDowall pronounced the old studio's epitaph: "It was the happiest place to make movies in all the world."

III. Screenplay

In emphasizing the importance of the screenplay, I should draw a vital distinction. I have never claimed what some writers inevitably claim, that the writer as an individual is more important than the director—though in some cases this may be true—but that the writing of any movie, including the contributions of the producer, the director and your Aunt Sally, is more important than the staging thereof. No director can make a good movie out of a bad script, though there have been many occasions when a bad director has butchered a good one, usually by rewriting it.

Of course, nothing I have to say here pertains to those writer-directors who can make a valid claim to authorship, a Chaplin, a Bergman, a Sturges, or their modern equivalents. But some critics and historians fail to draw distinctions; they make every director an Auteur, as does that pernicious credit, "A Film By," which implies sole authorship. When I wrote, produced and directed *The View from Pompey's Head*, the only author I could discern was Hamilton Basso, who wrote the novel.

At times in the past, I have been overcome by partisan passion to the extent of comparing the relationship of director to script to that of orchestra conductor to composition. That is, as Mozart's G minor Symphony as conducted by Bernstein or Ozawa would sound much the same to a layman, if not to a musician, so our movie would have looked much the same if it had been directed by Wyler instead of Ford.

I believe now that the analogy is false because it disregards the visual impact of what the director does, his tempos, moods, and choice of camera angles, and the types of performance he elicits from the actors. Parenthetically, I have always believed that there is as great a similarity between a movie and a musical composition as there is between a movie and a play. The variety in mood and tempo that can be created by lighting, effects and background music is far more significant on the screen than it can ever be on the stage, though some modern theater productions, such as *Nicholas Nickleby, Les Misérables* and *Sweeney Todd*, have gone in for quasi-cinematic techniques.

A more acceptable analogy of screenplay to finished picture would be that

16

of architect's blueprints to finished house. The entire house is forecast in the blueprints, its shape and structure in minute detail, but not the painting, the landscaping, the furnishing and to some extent the choice of materials which give the complete house its own distinctive style.

If style is the director's most obvious contribution—and it certainly would be in two directors as stylistically different as Wyler and Ford—that does not imply that the writer too doesn't impose his style on the finished structure. And this brings us directly to the function of the screenwriter, so often adapting the work of another writer that the style he (or she always being understood) imposes may not be entirely his (or her) own.

When I have talked with students at universities around the country, I have always emphasized two points: first, that character is far more important than plot, there being no new plots, but as many characters as there have been individuals since the first australopithecine decided that he (or she) preferred two feet to four; second, that in adapting a novel or play to the screen, the writer should make every effort to retain the original author's intent and style. (Of course, if the original author is the screenwriter himself, so much the better.) I broke this second rule only once: Ring Lardner, Jr. and I considered the novel *Forever Amber* to be ludicrous, and by great effort succeeded in making it merely irrelevant.

My screenplay of *How Green Was My Valley* contains very little dialogue that is mine, most of it in the love scenes between Angharad and Gruffydd. The style is clearly that of Richard Llewellyn, not my own. Yet in 1976, U.S. public television played a BBC mini-series of the same book which differs from my version as night from day. One critic, who apparently hadn't liked our movie (or perhaps hadn't seen it) remarked that the BBC production for the first time captured the style and essence of the novel—which was precisely what I had tried very hard to do.

How to explain such an anomaly? One explanation could be that it was a question of differing emphases: that I had emphasized aspects of the novel that the BBC adapters had not—and vice versa. However you explain it, one point stands out: that the difference between two adaptations of the same novel will always be infinitely greater than the difference between what two directors might do with the same screenplay. Precisely therein lies the importance of the screenwriter's contribution, even when he merely adapts another writer's original work. This is particularly true when a long novel such as *How Green Was My Valley* must be compressed into two hours or so of time on the screen. It is the screenplay, not the direction, which establishes the shape and structure of the movie, and also its dramatic essence.

For instance, seventeen years later, when I adapted John O'Hara's *Ten North Frederick* for my own direction, I based my screenplay on about forty pages of a four hundred page novel. Moreover, because censorship of the time forbade abortions, an abortion being an important story point, to get around this difficulty I was forced to write a series of original scenes in what I hoped was O'Hara's style—and he had an exquisite ear for language as it is spoken in the social circles he liked to write about. It was with some trepidation that I sent him the final screenplay—he was a close personal friend—but he approved it with a few minor suggestions, and years later in an interview, also approved the finished movie, adding that he had walked out on both *Butterfield Eight* and *From the Terrace*, both also adapted from his novels.

In 1949, I had a completely different problem with *David and Bathsheba*: how to flesh out the bare skeleton of a story told in the Second Book of Samuel, and do it with characters and dialogue which retained the flavor of the Old Testament, yet modernized, without indulgence in DeMillish vulgarisms and anachronisms. It is a condition of the craft that stylistically a screenwriter must be something of a chameleon. I was not Richard Llewellyn or John O'Hara, nor could I hope to be the elegant scholars of the King James version, but I had to sound like a reasonable facsimile of all. (However, cinematic historian Tom Stempel, in his excellent book about Nunnally Johnson, *Screenwriter*, did after a fashion credit me with idiosyncrasy of style by referring to my screenplays as "relentlessly literate.")

My introduction to *How Green Was My Valley* came early in 1940, and provides a perfect example of how two experienced screenwriters could take entirely different approaches to adapting the same book.

Zanuck sent me a complete screenplay by one of the deans of his writing staff, Ernest Pascal. My heart sank when I saw Pascal's name because I knew that I was being forced into the position of criticizing a fellow-writer's work, and he was not only a colleague but a friend and ally: we were both officers of the old Screen Writers Guild (he had recently been its president), which was then engaged in a bitter struggle for recognition by the studios, with Zanuck himself in violent opposition to the very idea of a writers' union, which he saw as a threat to his absolute authority.

When I called Ernie to tell him that I had his script he told me that I should say about it exactly what I thought, that it had had a poor reception in that long green office, and that he was sick of the whole project. I humbly thanked him, read the script, and told Zanuck that while it was beautifully written I found it so gloomy and depressing that I wondered what had prompted him to buy the rights to the novel in the first place. Zanuck's reply, characteristically succinct and to the point, was to send me a copy of the book, without comment.

I started to read the novel right after breakfast the next day, and stopped only when my wife took it from me by force and violence at midnight. I finished it the following day and spent another day writing a long memorandum to Zanuck, not only accepting the assignment but outlining how I thought the subject should be approached. (Zanuck never used the telephone; we communicated almost entirely by memo. When I would send him a memo, he would send it back with his reply typed on it in red ink. Unfortunately, when early in 1942 I took a leave of absence in order to enter government war service for the duration, most of my pre-war correspondence was lost.)

The gist of my memo was that I thought the Pascal script had emphasized the labor strife and the industrial ruin of the valley, while virtually ignoring the warm human comedy and tragedy which glowed on almost every page of the novel. I felt that the emphasis should be on the family, on the process of the boy Huw growing up and learning about life and love, as well as tragedy and death as he remembered it all in old age. The struggle of the miners to organize, the blackening of the green valley and the growing unemployment would serve only as catalysts for the gradual but irreversible

18

disintegration of the once happy, prosperous and closely-knit family.

It was about this time that I discovered that there had been an even earlier script, this one by Liam O'Flaherty, original author of the novel *The Informer*. I read it, hoping to find a few nuggets of wisdom in it, but in fact discovered that it was absolutely useless: one long revolutionary diatribe, with page-long speeches by presumably semi-literate miners. It must have driven Zanuck right up the wall.

When Mel Gussow's authorized biography of Zanuck, *Don't Say Yes Until I Finish Talking*, was published in 1971, and Darryl sent me a warmly autographed copy, I was startled to discover that two months before I sent him my memo he had sent one to Pascal making almost exactly the same points. In other words, from the beginning we had shared exactly the same vision for the movie, and arrived at it independently of each other. It was therefore no wonder that he instructed me to go ahead and write the screenplay, omitting the customary step of first submitting a "treatment."

But, also in the Gussow biography, Zanuck seriously misstated the case when he claimed that "we eliminated the most controversial element in the book, which was the labor and capital battle in connection with the strike." This is not only completely untrue, but in direct conflict with a statement he was making at the time, as reported to me by many happy scandal-mongers on the lot, that I had talked him "into making a goddam pro-labor picture." (This was absolute nonsense; nobody ever talked Darryl Zanuck into making anything he didn't want to make.)

I suppose that all of us who rely on memory—and I don't exclude myself—will sometimes proclaim as fact something we fondly wish had been the case. So it must have been with Darryl. The fact is that, far from being eliminated, the "labor and capital battle" set off the most serious family quarrel, between the union-minded sons and the conservative father, which resulted in the boys actually leaving the house and rooming elsewhere. "Are we sheep?" cried Ianto, "to be herded and sheared by a handful of owners?" I resolved the dispute in my script by having the preacher Gruffydd, who had been a socialist firebrand in earlier scripts, act as a sort of umpire and render final judgment in the line: "First, have your union. You need it. Alone you are weak. Together you are strong. But remember that with strength goes responsibility—to others and to yourselves. For you cannot conquer injustice with more injustice—only with justice and with the help of God." This was the definitive political statement made in our movie.

Darryl accepted it as a compromise, though it accurately expressed my own views. I also used the line to advance the story: it moved Angharad to say to Gruffydd, "Will we always be in your debt? Now you have made us a family again," thus triggering our most effective love scene.

Yet, strangely enough, the line lent credence to Zanuck's claim that I had talked him into making "a goddam pro-labor picture." Innocuous as it may sound today, in 1941, when the picture was released, it was a daring and even radical statement. At that time, the very right of labor to organize was a hot political issue. The great sit-down strikes were still vivid in memory, the beatings of union organizers by Henry Ford's goons, and the persecution of the Okies in California's San Joaquin Valley.

And the supreme irony of all was that this pro-union statement was hammered out in civilized discussion by two men who were not only on opposite political sides, but in active personal confrontation, for Darryl was still adamantly opposed to the very idea of a writers' union, and I was vice-president of the union he opposed.

I can't help thinking that if I had been Zanuck I wouldn't have been kicking myself for having made a pro-labor picture, nor congratulating myself for eliminating the issue, but rather taking credit for being the great producer he was, able to put aside his own prejudices and let the movie say what it had to say, just as he had done with the far more radical 1940 *The Grapes of Wrath*.

When John Ford had begun to catch a lot of right-wing flak for having directed *The Grapes of Wrath*, he had wired me from New York asking me for an excuse for having made the picture. I had wired back two words: "The picture." The right-wing extremists were probably correct in picking on *The Grapes of Wrath*. To them, it was the more offensive of the pictures for two reasons: first, Tom Joad's poetic final speech, made by a man forced by "the system" into a radical underground; second, because in *How Green Was My Valley*, while we attacked the mine-owners for their greed and came down hard on the side of the union, we also frowned on the violent tactics of union extremists in stoning Morgan's house and threatening his person, this leading to his wife's fiery defense and, if indirectly, to the crippling of Huw. We showed both sides, *The Grapes of Wrath* only one.

In 1940, momentous events in Europe were directly affecting our movie. Zanuck, one of whose most endearing characteristics was his ability to inspire enthusiasm in his apostles, had projected for me a colossal *How Green Was My Valley*, which would have been our answer to the reigning colossus, *Gone With the Wind*. I was to write a four-hour picture, which would be shot in gorgeous Technicolor on location in Wales with an all-star cast.

In August, one bubble burst with the beginning of the Battle of Britain. South Wales, Britain's principal source of coal, was a primary target for Hitler's Luftwaffe, and all plans to shoot on location there had to be scrapped. A location in the hills behind Malibu was suggested by the art department. I flew over it in a light plane to inspect it, immediately realized that the dull olive chaparral of arid Southern California could never substitute for the vivid green of rain-swept Cwm Rhondda, and wrote Zanuck a memo regretfully suggesting that the idea of shooting in color should also be scrapped. Back came in red ink word that the decision to scrap it had already been made. All this had some effect on my screenplay: scenes that I had planned for the Welsh location were rewritten to play in our village street set or on sound stages.

For a while, there were no further significant changes. Unlike some producers, Zanuck didn't require his writers to turn in a quota of pages every week. Once the assignment was made, he left you severely alone. In 1946, for instance, I spent six weeks in the desert writing *The Ghost and Mrs. Muir* without so much as a memo or a phone call from either Zanuck or staff producer Fred Kohlmar. You were trusted to get the job done.

I must have done a prodigious amount of work between 15 July, when I started on the screenplay, and 23 August, when I turned in my first draft, timed for about four hours on the screen, as I had been instructed. Actually, my task was made infinitely easier because I was able to use much of Llewellyn's dialogue without change. It all "played," as we say, not always the case with novelists' material, and certainly he knew better than I how the people in a Welsh mining community would talk.

Having sent the script off to be mimeographed, I thought I wouldn't be hearing from Zanuck for a few days, and would have time for some politics. Specifically, as an officer of the Democratic State Central Committee, I was scheduled to chair a fund-raising luncheon honoring Secretary of Agriculture Henry A. Wallace, who had been picked by Franklin D. Roosevelt as his new vice-presidential running mate in that election year.

The luncheon was rudely interrupted by Republican Zanuck, whose secretary had successfully tracked me down at the old Ambassador Hotel. When I was called from the head table to answer the phone, he asked me: "Where the hell are you?" I answered: "Oh, I'm here at the Ambassador introducing the next vice-president of the United States." "Well," said he, "this is the vice-president in charge of production at Twentieth Century-Fox, and I'm calling to tell you that your script is twice too long. Come and see me tomorrow." Another bubble had burst, and my colossus was shrinking fast. However, as I hung up I reflected that he must have liked the script, since I was still assigned to the picture.

The next day I found out that he liked about half of the script, since he wanted to cut it in half, but it wasn't clear to me—nor, I suspect, to him—just what he wanted cut. He told me to go over the entire script, cutting what I could, and he would do the same, after which we would compare notes. Such indecision was not characteristic.

For a few days I glumly struggled with the problem of which arm, which leg to sacrifice. The proper surgical solution was staring me in the face, but I stubbornly refused to see it: the boy Huw should never be allowed to grow up. It never occurred to me because the studio's reigning male star, Tyrone Power, was scheduled to play the adult Huw.

I was naturally somewhat aggrieved because I had been told to write a four-hour movie and was now being attacked for it. What I didn't know at the time, but which now seems obvious, was that Darryl himself was under attack, in this case by the hard-eyed money men known collectively to us toilers in the Hollywood vineyard by the pejorative cognomen "New York." Years later, a different set of money men—but still "New York"—managed to install their own man as chief of production at Twentieth Century-Fox, and he summed up his opinion of my screenplay for *Ten North Frederick* in the bleak phrase: "I don't like tragedies." And that, I believe, is how the 1940 money men looked on a story which recounted the decline of a culture, the disintegration of a family, and ended with the death of one of its leading characters. This was no glitzy *Gone With the Wind, The Wizard of Oz* or *Meet Me in St. Louis.* Even *The Grapes of Wrath* had ended on a note of hope.

Then Zanuck played an ace. Bypassing his own stable of directors, he borrowed from Sam Goldwyn the hottest director in town, the youthful but already famous William Wyler.

IV. Preparation

In 1934, I had lunch one day at Universal Studios with Preston Sturges, and we went on the set of *The Good Fairy*, which he had adapted from Ferenc Molnar's play, to call on another friend of mine, Margaret Sullavan. She introduced me to her director and soon-to-be husband, William Wyler, and thus was born a friendship which ended only with Willy's death in 1981, when I had the melancholy honor of delivering the eulogy at his memorial service in our Directors Guild theater.

Perhaps a few of the things I said about him on that sad occasion will bear repeating. I spoke of his courage under fire as an Army Air Corps officer in World War II, when he flew many missions over Nazi Germany to make his matchless combat documentary, *The Memphis Belle*, and of another kind of courage, when he stood up for the rights of an unpopular minority during the evil time of the Hollywood blacklist. To quote from my eulogy: "And he brought this courage to his professional career. Any member of this Guild can tell you that the hardest part of the job is to take the time you need to get the scene right—and that means resisting the ferocious pressures of the front office to hurry up, save money, stay on some pipe-dream schedule. Nobody, not Sam Goldwyn, not Y. Frank Freeman, not the multiple moguls at Metro-Goldwyn-Mayer, could force Willy to hurry, to skimp, to turn in a shoddy piece of work. Nor could the actors whom Willy drove—some say without mercy—until they finally achieved the perfection he demanded. His favorite line was 'You can do it better'—and nobody left that sound stage until everyone, including Willy himself, had done his very best. If he was tough on others, he was twice as tough on himself."

I expected my screenplay to be subjected to the same trial by fire, and so it was. We spent weeks going over every scene, every line, playing out the scenes for each other, making notes for business. Substantively, we changed very little, though in scene after scene there were subtle improvements, a cut, an added dimension, a stronger emotion, proving again and again that always "You can do it better."

Darryl Zanuck, much to his chagrin, was left out of the process. Willy had insisted that the Dunnes and Wylers should escape the imperium on Pico Boulevard and work at the lovely mountain resort of Arrowhead Springs. (He and Maggie Sullavan were now divorced, and he had married Margaret Tallichet, who remains to this day one of our best friends.) If Darryl left writers alone to write and directors to direct, he feared conspiracy and possible mutiny when the two managed to wriggle out together from under his benevolent thumb. He called us separately every day, sometimes in the middle of the night, when he was sure he would catch each of us alone. He warned me of Willy's extravagance and Willy of my politics. We took turns assuring him that we were making no substantive changes, radical or otherwise, nor adding to the cost.

But in one respect, we dismally failed, we were supposed to cut the script, but Willy rejected all Zanuck's suggestions for eliminations, and even mine. Actually, we spent most of our time juggling the continuity. We had so many stories to tell that they tended to stumble over each other: if we followed one too closely, we interfered with the flow of the others. If we broke it up, the picture would seem jumpy and disorganized. Our job would have been made much easier had we known that three of the sequences we juggled, which Willy and I considered vital to our story, were eliminated in the final editing stages. A lot of expensive celluloid then festooned the cutting-room floor.

We returned from Arrowhead Springs with a script that was tighter and improved, but not much shorter, and nobody, not even Zanuck, seemed to know what to do about it. We were now in the pre-production phase. Sets were being designed, locations in the Malibu hills pin-pointed. Zanuck assigned top-notch professionals to the key production jobs: Gregg Toland as cameraman, Richard Day and Nathan Juran as art directors, James B. Clark as film editor. Alfred Newman, in charge of all Twentieth Century-Fox music, would do the score. The process of casting the picture was begun. It would have been hard to find enough qualified Welsh actors in Hollywood for our entire cast, and Zanuck and the movie's two directors who, seriatim, worked on casting with him, wound up with a mixed bag of Welsh, Irish, Scots, English, Canadian and American performers. When Wyler and I discussed possible cast, we knew that we could always find capable people for the adult parts. Our problem was to unearth a new and exciting child actor to play Huw, who would have to carry so much of our story. And, hovering over us like a black cloud was the knowledge that our script was still much too long—and none of us knew how to cut it.

Then manna fell from Heaven, in a way that solved both our problems at once. The manna took the shape of a twelve-year-old actor named Roddy McDowall. His father, a retired British merchant marine officer, who, with his country at war, was going back to sea, had recently moved his family to New York. Two weeks after they arrived, young Roddy answered a call from Metro-Goldwyn-Mayer, which was testing boys for *The Yearling*. The casting people there decided he was too British, but suggested he try 20th Century-Fox over on Tenth Avenue, where they were testing young Britons for *How Green Was My Valley*.

The rest is history. When we ran the New York test out on the Coast, we knew at once that we had found our Huw. Not only that, but at a stroke the boy also solved our length problem: this Huw should never be permitted to grow up. (We all have taken credit for being the first to say it—I think the truth is that the idea hit us all simultaneously.)

It took me only a few days to make the cuts. Two sequences were retained which had featured the adult Huw: his scene with Angharad when she returns to the valley after her marriage has ended in disaster, and the final sequence in the movie, in which he accompanies preacher Gruffydd and blind pugilist Dai Bando down into the flooded mine in search of his father. Magically, both sequences played much better with a boy of twelve than with a man ten years older.

Strangely enough, by cutting out his adult life we made Huw even more the real star of the picture than he had been before. Discussing this, Willy and I agreed that neither of us had realized, before we found this perfect Huw, how essential it was to our story that he should be perfect. Without him, we would have had much less of a picture. As for Tyrone Power, he told me that he was much relieved not to be asked to star in half a movie. And I'm certain that he realized—as most actors do—that it is sure death on the screen to be forced into any sort of competition with a child, let alone to replace one.

My screenplay was now officially slugged "Final," and I said goodbye to it with few regrets. I was happy that at last we had found our star, and that my work (and Llewellyn's) would be in the hands of a producer who respected it, and a director who had helped to shape it in its final form. (As Willy would later remark, he didn't subscribe to the Auteur theory, though, having been born in Alsace, he was the only American director who could pronounce it.) Fat, dumb and happy, as the pilots say, I retired with my wife for some rest and recreation to a beautiful ranch owned by connections of hers in the Santa Ynez Valley. Then "New York" struck.

Willy called me at the ranch to inform me that he was packing up and returning to Sam Goldwyn. When I hotfooted it back to the studio, Zanuck filled in the details. The money men in New York hated the script, hated the lack of big name stars in our cast, were scared stiff by the Wyler reputation for extravagance, and thus, in a fresh demonstration of their customary impeccable judgment, had decided that the movie would be a disaster and refused to authorize the money for it.

Darryl didn't take this lying down. He informed me that he had told them that this was the finest script he had ever had, that somehow, by hook or by crook, he was going to make this movie, even if it meant a deal with some other studio. I appreciated the sentiment, but still found it hard to believe that our project was not completely dead.

It was with something like broken hearts that my wife and I—as usual I had involved Amanda and her fine mind in every act of the drama—took off to go fishing in the Bahamas. I wanted to get as far away from the studio as possible. I felt, like Prospero in *The Tempest,* that our revels now were ended, and that our actors, sets, locations and the script itself were melted into air, into thin air, leaving not a rack behind. Every writer must learn to survive rejections emotionally unscathed, but this one, to me, was the brutal stamping out by the jackboots of the money men of what had become a genuine labor of love.

V. Production

When Jim Pepper set me to writing these notes, he set himself the more arduous task of doing the necessary research—necessary in part because my prewar files had been lost. I merely had to fish in the depths of my memory, somewhat roiled after fifty years, but he had to spend hours in university libraries, the Motion Picture Academy, bookstores which deal in still photographs of old movies, poring over the incredible amount of paper generated by the production of any movie.

I was absolutely stunned by one of his discoveries. I had always assumed that at least two years had elapsed from the time I was first introduced to the Llewellyn novel and the actual start of production, with several months passing between the apparent abandonment of the project and its reinstatement. The research proved that in fact less than a year after I first read the novel we were in production, and that our time in purgatory was a mere matter of weeks.

In January 1941, I was summoned to the long green office and there sat my old friend Jack Ford, chewing on his handkerchief and greeting me with the insults which in our culture are the essential lingua franca of boon companionship. I was happy that he also insulted my script, a sure sign of his approval.

I was delighted to see him for several reasons: first, because it meant that we were back on track, second because I admired his work, last but not least because we had been friends for ten years.

I had first met him in late 1930 on the set of his *Seas Beneath* at the old Fox Studio on Western Avenue. At the time, he was a lordly director and I a lowly reader, but he let no such social distinctions stand between us. We were both Irish history buffs, and we revelled in the legendary exploits of Finn Mac-Cool and Cuchulainn, the darker realities inflicted on Ireland by the injustices and cruelties of Cromwell and Castlereagh, and the heroics of Robert Emmet and Michael Collins.

Some of these learned discussions took place aboard the "Araner," his seagoing ketch which usually lay anchored off Catalina Island, on evenings which were damp inside and out—fog without and Irish whiskey within.

Much has been written about Ford's Homeric bouts with the bottle. It is true that he could and did drink, but what is usually left out is that he lived and worked in an age in which alcoholic excess was common, especially among the governing classes: bankers and captains of industry in New York, undergraduates in the Ivy League colleges, writers, actors, directors on Broadway or in Hollywood, even in the halls of Congress, where legislators from the Bible Belt who voted Dry matched their Wet colleagues from the more openly bibulous Northeast, belt for belt. Hypocrisy, our national vice, truly flowered under Prohibition.

"Work," we sang, "is the curse of the drinking classes," and English satirist Hilaire Belloc summed it all up in a couplet: "Like many of the Upper Class / He liked the sound of broken glass." Then there was the Emerald Bay Yacht Club, an organization which had no connection whatever with the sea and whose sole function was to hold an annual dinner on St. Patrick's Day, "Commodore" John Ford presiding. Grandson Dan Ford, in his biography, *Pappy*, describes our last dinner, shortly before *How Green Was My Valley* went into production, and nine months before America went to war. It was held at "The House of Murphy," an Irish restaurant in Hollywood. Among those present were veteran directors Frank Borzage and Tay Garnett, actors Frank Morgan, Johnny Weissmuller and Preston Foster, writers Liam O'Flaherty and Dudley Nichols, and members of Jack's intimate circle, such as Wingate Smith, John Wayne, Harry Wurtzel and Ward Bond. Dan Ford reports, I fear with some accuracy, that everyone proceeded to get speechlessly drunk.

But all play and no work would have made Jack a dull boy indeed, and there was no thought of the cup that cheers once the picture was under way.

A peculiar circumstance I must now reveal, and that is that I had little direct contact with Ford after the first meeting in Zanuck's office, which was purely introductory. It may be that Darryl, still smarting from the Wyler experience, deliberately kept us apart, but I think that the true explanation is that Jack preferred to work alone, and that he loved to spring surprises on his co-workers. When, eight years later, we were once more teamed up on *Pinky*, we had very few meetings, and Lamar Trotti had a similar experience on *Young Mr. Lincoln*. Other writers have confirmed to me that Ford was equally secretive with them.

I had never worked with him before, and when, after that first meeting, I heard nothing for several days, I went to see him. He asked me if I was one of those writers who have to be told how wonderful they are every day. I replied that, since I was now back on the assembly line, and on deadline on another assignment, I merely wanted to know if he had any brilliant directorial touches to suggest. He said he hadn't, and then—as if on an afterthought—"Oh, make the other prizefighter a sort of second or handler for Dai Bando, and I'll throw the part to that poor bastard Barry Fitzgerald, who can't get a job."

The only other meeting we had of which I have any memory was with Zanuck late in January. We confirmed the casting of Fitzgerald and made some minor cuts and changes, along with a major one: the scene between the two children, Huw and Ceinwen, vaguely hinting at forthcoming sexuality. Poor Ceinwen, who had been the main love interest of the grownup Huw in my first script, later received the coup de grâce when her only other substantial scene wound up on the cutting-room floor.

About the actual shooting of the picture, all my information is secondhand, since I was on the set only four times, and only once saw rushes, and that time by pure accident. I had booked a projection room, and was still there making notes after the lights went up, when an assistant cutter brought in that day's rushes to prepare for Zanuck. Naturally, I succumbed to temptation and stayed.

What I saw horrified me. They were shooting the wedding celebration, and Ford had Donald Crisp as Gwilym Morgan singing an obviously Irish drinking song. Like Byron's Sennacherib, I came down on the set like the wolf on the fold, but Ford soon defanged the wolf with a bit of blarney and a nonchalant: "Ah, go on! The Welsh are just another lot of micks and biddies, only Protestants." Jack did much the same sort of thing to the Navy brass during World War II. He broke every rule in their tidy little Annapolis book, shunned "officer country" to consort with enlisted men, and in return they made the ersatz "Commodore" of the Emerald Bay Yacht Club a genuine Rear Admiral, U.S.N.R.

Until the picture was finished, edited, scored and ready to be shipped, I never saw another foot of film. That was the major problem with being a writer on the assembly line, even at "the writers' studio."

The next time I visited the set was by invitation, to rewrite a line. Ford was shooting the first school sequence, in which the teacher sends Huw to sit on the dunce's stool. When they finished the rehearsal, Jack said to me: "See that? See how the kid sort of felt for the stool with his ass while keeping his eyes on the teacher? I didn't tell him to do that. He just naturally does everything right the first time."

My next visit to the set came when my wife was lunching with me in the studio commissary and Ford spotted her. She had always been a great favorite of his. When Amanda Duff of Santa Barbara was signed by the studio out of the New York stage hit *Tovarich*, in which she had been the ingenue lead, she was told to visit sets and so familiarize herself with movie-making. She decided

26

she preferred Ford's *Four Men and a Prayer* set to any other, and he had a stool set up for her just behind the camera. So now, after asking her why she had sunk so low as to marry a writer, he invited her to drop by the set, generously adding that it was okay if she wanted to drag her husband along too. When we got there, he had a stool ready for her, right behind the camera. He also had the cast and crew lined up to sing, to the tune of *The Farmer in the Dell*: "We haven't changed a line / We haven't changed a line / It's just the way you wrote it / We haven't changed a line." Knowing Jack, I suspected him of trying to tell me: "Naturally we've made a few changes, but only minor ones." As I would learn later, there was one major change: an entire scene rewritten for a retake.

My fourth and last visit came when the cantankerous Sara Allgood as Beth Morgan kicked up a fuss over the tutoring scene, when she scoffs at the notion of trying to fill a tub full of holes. According to Jack, she claimed that the scene didn't play, but he winked at me as he said it. I remembered a story that he had once replied to a producer who had complained that he was behind schedule by tearing ten pages out of his script and saying, "Now I'm on schedule." So I tore the offending page out of his script and said, "Now it plays." Jack told Sally Allgood that since the son-of-a-bitching writer wouldn't help them, they'd have to play the scene exactly as it was—which of course was what he had wanted in the first place.

That is the sum of my direct connection with the production phase. When Zanuck finally showed me the completed picture, my mind was a perfect tabula rasa, innocent of preconceived opinions, except one: I knew that what I would see would be well directed. The difference was that if Willy Wyler had directed, I would have known exactly what to expect, because we had played out the entire movie many times over. I simply had no idea how Ford would handle the same material.

In one way, the two directors were very much alike. Some directors belong to the one-two-three-kick school: they add nothing of visual excitement in their choice of camera angles and mood in lighting, or any real spark to the performances. Yet many such have plodded their way into lucrative careers. On the other extreme are the look-ma-no-hands types, the directors who constantly call attention to themselves with weird angles, unmotivated camera moves, visible focus changes and other ploys to remind you that the Wizard of Oz is back there behind the camera, cleverly juggling his devices. Too many critics too often applaud such directorial showoffs.

The really great directors, such as Ford and Wyler (I'll mention no more, for fear of leaving someone out) shun such shoddy strategies, but at the same time they know every trick of the trade, and how to use each to the greatest effect. Their supreme trick is to reveal no trick at all, to completely efface themselves while exploiting to the full the capabilities of the camera.

It was once said of the great English librettist W.S. Gilbert that he wrote what he pleased and it happened to rhyme. So it could be said of Wyler and Ford that in their movies the camera just happened to be in exactly the right place in every scene, and the actors just happened to get it right. The greatest compliment you can pay any director—or writer for that matter—is to forget that he exists. The critic who believed that Ann Sothern dreamed up her own dialogue was unintentionally paying the writer he had scorned just such a compliment.

I knew Ford's work would be good, but not how good, especially since I also knew that he had agreed to shoot the movie on a limited budget and at an unlimited pace. To put it in numbers, in eight weeks he brought in a picture that under normal conditions would have taken at least twelve. He accomplished this by "camera-cutting." What you see on the screen is practically all that was shot.

First of all, I was stunned by the movie's visual impact. Aided by the brilliant photography of Arthur Miller, who had replaced Gregg Toland when the picture was rescheduled, Jack transformed our humdrum California hills into an image of Wales that needed no color. Then there was the imaginative use of music, dominated by a Welsh choir discovered by music director Alfred Newman.

But even more important was the human element, the portrayal of this warm, close-knit family, devastated by physical and economic disaster, but clinging throughout to its courage and its hope. The warp and woof of comedy and tragedy were expertly knit into a single glowing tapestry of drama, and the frame that held it all in place was the superlative performance of a boy of twelve. Roddy McDowall proved to be all that we had hoped for, and more.

Second, there were many surprises, as I had suspected there would be, and most of them were pleasant. I have already mentioned the wonderful touch of the boy singing his way to his dying father in the flooded mine, and this was prepared for in a lovely moment during the opening sequence when Angharad and Huw sing a greeting to each other across the mountainside.

Barry Fitzgerald as Cyfartha turned out to be a stroke of casting genius, giving us moments of visual comedy in our basically tragic story. In particular, Jack had improved on the sequence in which the prize-fighter beats up the teacher (which I used to call my fascist sequence) by having Dai Bando, playing professor, address the frightened children instead of the man he was beating up. He added a wonderful closing line for Cyfartha: "No aptitude for knowledge."

In several scenes, Jack had used his camera to make an important point far better than I had made it in my script. When Ivor's choir is rehearsing in front of the house, he had the first two boys who were forced to leave home steal with their knapsacks out the back, while the camera held the crippled Huw in his bed in the far background. There was no need for a closeup to punch up this eloquent long shot. Audiences could imagine for themselves how Huw felt.

Jack achieved one of the most powerful effects in the movie by a similar imaginative use of the camera in the scene of Angharad's marriage to Iestyn Evans. First, whereas I had had the miners and their families celebrating the wedding as usual, he played the crowd silent and glum. Then he gave Morgan a stern line to Dai Bando: "Is there to be no singing for my daughter's wedding?" Only then did the people reluctantly sing.

As the married couple drove away in their carriage, I had had Huw look into the chapel and see Gruffydd methodically putting away his prayer-book, etc., establishing that he personally had performed the ceremony. Jack did far better. As the carriage pulled away, he simply had Gruffydd emerge in long shot from the back of the chapel, looking after it. Again, we needed no closeup. Besides, by a stroke of the luck that attends the work of good directors, a vagrant gust of wind caught Angharad's veil and whirled it high over her head. It was a magical pictorial moment, as well as one of powerful emotion, with the magnificent voices of the Welsh choir in the background.

There were a few negatives, some of them, I think, because Jack had to work so fast. When Huw crawls home after his savage whipping at the hands of the teacher, he meets his brothers, who are naturally dismayed by his plight. One of them cries out: "He has cut you to the bone, man!" Then Ianto picks him up and swings his naked back directly into the camera—without a mark on it.

I thought that it was a big mistake in the early scene when father and sons wash up to have Beth casually dump a bucket of water over her husband as he sits in a tub, peacefully smoking his pipe. It always gets a big laugh, but it is a cheap laugh because it is completely out of character. In that time and place, a man was master of his house, with all the dignity and authority of a biblical Abraham, or the *gravitas* of a Roman *paterfamilias*. I thought when I saw it that thereafter the audience might lose respect for Morgan. Fortunately, I was wrong.

There were other minor moments which struck me as wrong. When Huw walks again, one of our climactic scenes, I thought it was all too easy: little pain, little fear, no feeling that those frozen legs had been long months in bed.

There was some overplaying by bit actors, but that has been true of most Ford movies. Perhaps it was his lifelong sympathy for the underdog at work, his way of giving some little fellow his moment of full attention.

Jack invented a line for Cyfartha when blind Dai Bando is about to go down into the flooded mine: " 'Tis a coward I am—but I will hold your coat." The second half of the line is sheer genius, but the first half strikes me as completely false. I don't believe that any man will publicly dub himself a coward. He might say that he is afraid, but I think it would have been better if he had said, perhaps with a shudder as an explosion rumbles from below: "Down there is not for me—but I will hold your coat."

There was one scene which was beautifully played, but I completely disagreed with the physical action and mood: the scene where Gruffydd finds a lovelorn Angharad late at night in his house. Wyler and I had spent much time over this, because it was a love scene in which the woman is the aggressor, an idea usually considered more suitable for comedy than for drama. When we played it out, it was always with Angharad, sick with longing for him, as the dialogue explicitly indicates, moving towards Gruffydd, he on the defensive, trying to make her understand, always maintaining physical distance between them. The stage directions I wrote are also explicit on this point.

Ford completely ignored them. Possibly in his macho choreography of the dance of life the male invariably leads, the female follows. Whatever his reasoning, he had Gruffydd moving towards her throughout the scene, actually putting his hands on her and holding her. In fact, the scene ends in a tender embrace, effective in its way, but also completely reversing the character of this wild, tempestuous girl who had done the unthinkable when she in her desperation had come to a man's lodging in the middle of the night. She simply gives up, which is not the Angharad Llewellyn wrote. I couldn't help thinking, when I saw the scene, that once Gruffydd put his hands on her our Angharad would have forced a passionate and probably irrevocable embrace.

The scene as Jack shot it gave us sorrow and tenderness, but no sense whatever of sexuality.

I had only one really unpleasant surprise; one sequence had been dropped and replaced by a completely new one that I had not written. If Zanuck's assembly line system was to work as far as the writer was concerned, the inviolability of the script was essential. In this one case, the unwritten code was ignored, and so was I. It never happened to me before or since.

The sequence in question was the inception of Iestyn's courtship of Angharad. I had followed the book in having Ianto knock Iestyn down outside the chapel for daring to speak to Angharad. Iestyn's father, the mineowner, threatens Ianto with the law, but when he discovers that his son has actually violated custom and morality by speaking to the girl, he says: "If a man spoke to Iestyn's sister, murder would be done," and pushes his son into asking permission of Morgan to speak to his daughter. This leads Beth directly to the tearful line: "Too young—even to be thinking of marriage."

Zanuck had always hated the scene, saying that he didn't understand it, which was producer lingo for opining that audiences wouldn't understand this weird Welsh custom. Just because Ianto knocks Iestyn down for speaking to his sister, and Iestyn then asks the girl's father for permission, what's that got to do with marriage? I had vigorously defended the scene as self-explanatory, as clever story-telling, and also as good comedy.

Our disagreement may have been the reason why I wasn't consulted on the retake—my scene had actually been shot, as Jim Pepper discovered in his research—but I still deeply resented the lack of consideration on the part of both producer and director. It was another reminder that, even at "the writers' studio," we were still considered interchangeable if not expendable, and even to some extent were thought of as what a producer at another studio had called writers: "the help."

But I don't think that another writer had been sneaked in behind my back. In a memo to Ford of 10 July, 1941, Zanuck mentions a new comedy scene that will replace "the scene outside the church," with the clear indication that Jack would wing it on the set, and that seems to be what happened. What he accomplished was simply not up to the high standard he had set for himself in the rest of the picture. Once more, character was sacrificed for cheap laughs.

If there is one axiom in dramatic writing, it is that character should never be compromised. Drama has been defined as the reaction of character to crisis. Character should drive the action, never be distorted by it. In this unfortunate retake, the latter is precisely what occurred.

It began brilliantly with a bit of good coarse horseplay, in which Huw's legs are being massaged by his brothers, and Angharad offends his dignity "as a man," by lifting the towel to slap him on the rump, a wonderful invention. Then the scene deteriorates fast. Morgan, who has been soaking his feet in a tub, answers the door and there is the mineowner, come to ask permission for his son to speak to his employee's daughter.

So far so good: the father parading in bare feet before his boss while he considers this request. If they'd left it at that, they still would have had a good scene, funny enough because the proud father has to perform his judicious function in his bare feet, while his wife seriously mistimes her entrance with his

30

shoes. But they had the entire Morgan family not only respectful to the boss, but actually servile. Morgan bows and scrapes; Beth comes simpering in with the shoes, gazing adoringly on Evans; the militant union leaders Ianto and Davy hide their pipes like guilty schoolboys; Morgan himself seems to be apologizing for his pride when he is given the totally unnecessary line, "We're a very proud family," when that pride underlies the entire situation.

What really puzzles me is how Jack could have got the relationship so wrong, when obviously he got it exactly right when he shot the original scene. We have mute witnesses to this in the surviving set stills. Still photographers customarily recreate the action by posing the actors in the scene's climactic moments, and here we have Ianto knocking down the boss's son, then pointing at him in scornful condemnation ("That's where he was. Buttonhole and all.") while Morgan stands, stern and ramrod straight, confronting the mineowner himself. As for Beth, the stills don't show it, but in my scene, true to Llewellyn, her reaction to Iestyn's courtship was so far from simpering as to protest vehemently that Angharad is too young.

The entire scene as shot is completely out of character, and I still wince when I see it. At least it ends on a legitimate laugh: Morgan sneezes, and his solemn sons chorus "God bless you."

So much for the negatives. As for the performances, I felt—and still feel—that most of them are wonderful: Roddy McDowall, Donald Crisp as Morgan (except in that one scene), Rhys Williams and Barry Fitzgerald as Dai Bando and Cyfartha, all the boys, but especially John Loder as the proud Ianto, and those two superb "women of the green valley," as they would later call themselves, Maureen O'Hara and Anna Lee.

Walter Pidgeon makes a perfectly acceptable Gruffydd, but when I watch him I'm always conscious that I'm in the presence of a Hollywood leading man, not quite a preacher who has worked his way up through the mines. He provided a touch of the glamor that we needed, but so did Maureen O'Hara, who at the same time is utterly convincing as a miner's daughter.

My biggest disappointment was Sarah Allgood. Donald Crisp won an Academy Award for his performance as Morgan, and the part of Beth I always thought was even stronger. When I heard that the great Sally Allgood of the Abbey Theater was to play it, I thought that she would steal the picture. She had it in her hands, and she blew it. She had three of the best lines in the show (key lines can be important in determining awards), but she threw them all away.

When Morgan offers Huw money for every bruise and scrape he incurs fighting in school, including a broken nose, she interjects, "fiercely" according to my stage direction, "Break your old nose then! Break your mother's heart every time you go from the house!" This is aimed not at the boy, but at his father. It is a direct confrontation, a questioning of his authority, far more serious a matter than dousing his pipe with a bucket of water. It is an expression of the age-old differences between man and woman over the raising of a child. On the screen, it comes off as none of these, merely as a petulance.

Beth has a marvelous mystic line of Llewellyn's when Huw is trying to show her where her sons are scattered over the world: "I know where they are . . . they are in the house." I had written the stage direction "flatly," but I certainly didn't intend the kind of flatness with which Sally Allgood read it.

Perhaps the most powerful line in the entire movie was hers in the poignant scene after her son Ivor has been killed and her grandson born to the new widow, Bronwen. Morgan says piously, "Give one, take the other," and she responds, "fiercely" according to the stage direction: "Go to that girl up by there and say that to her." "Hisht, now, Beth," says Morgan, shocked, "Do not kindle the wrath." She replies, "To hell with the wrath!" She raises her eyes directly to heaven and adds: "And I said it plain to be heard!"

This should have had all the power and passion of the dying Beethoven shaking his fist at a lowering sky. It is a direct and unequivocal defiance and daring of her God, in this deeply religious family, a deliberate and naked blasphemy. I had had to negotiate a special waiver from the industry's internal censorship for the line, including the word "hell," which was then forbidden by the Code. What is more, I had intended it to pave the way for her line at the end of the picture when she senses that her husband is dead and tells Angharad of "the glory" he has seen. I was trying to show that at last she was at peace with her God, and her blasphemy forgiven. But there had been no blasphemy; the line was thrown away casually as she exited the scene.

The last thing I would have expected of Jack Ford was to let her underplay that scene as she did. Perhaps he was afraid of all its implications, or perhaps he simply didn't understand it. Perhaps the reason was even more superficial. He didn't like Sally Allgood and didn't hesitate to tell me so, in language that would blister this page. A member of the cast told me that she was the one truly discordant member of the company: she got on with nobody. It was really a shame. It would have been wonderful to have won the other major award for which the picture was eligible. (That is, besides the screenplay award, which—to my great personal chagrin—it also didn't get.)

I hope that in detailing the negatives, I haven't diluted the impact of the movie on me, then and now. I felt that Ford had done a powerful, imaginative and poetic job, and my disagreements all together add up to only an extremely small part of my reaction.

But I did learn from it an important truth: none of the key people involved in any movie should be excluded from any part of the process. A gifted producer like Darryl Zanuck could get away with running an assembly line, and perhaps he couldn't work in any other way, but writers should not be barred from the set—or at least from seeing rushes—nor directors from the writing and the editing.

All of us, writers, directors, producers and actors, can make mistakes. The best assurance that errors can be detected and corrected is the availability of other professionals. None of us should ever forget that a movie, like any successful stage play—or for that matter Chartres Cathedral and the King James Version of the Bible—is, or should be, a collaboration.

VI. Aftermath

I have never believed that writing can be taught in classrooms, but it is true that negatives can be taught. Aspiring writers can be given a list of "don'ts":

for instance, never leave a room (or a scene) by the same door through which you came in. In other words, every scene should somehow advance your story. My post-production experience on this movie provided a case in point.

After that first screening, I was on my way back to my office, still somewhat dazed by the wonders I had seen, when it suddenly occurred to me that great chunks of my screenplay were missing, sequences that I had always considered important, and that had survived all revisions.

There were two scenes at Gruffydd's lathe, in which Huw's mentor gives him a pencil-box, along with some solid advice on living, the true nature of poverty and wealth, sorrow and happiness. There was the tailor-shop scene in which Huw gets long trews—Welsh for trousers—for the first time, thereby leading to his initial speculations on the subject of sex. There was the scene in which Huw, jealous of the widowed Bronwen's new suitor, cons the rather dim fellow into abandoning the chase.

In each case, the cuts had cost us something. When the school bully smashes the pencil-box, we don't know why this is important to Huw—though it really isn't important to our story. In the tailor-shop scene, we lost—besides some wonderful comedy—the introduction of the adolescent boy to the mysteries of sex. In the scene in which Huw gulls the suitor, we lost a sort of leit-motif in our story: Huw's lifelong love for Bronwen, conceived in the moment he first saw her when he was a child, and never thereafter relinquished. In my screenplay, at the end of the suitor scene the old Huw summed it up in his narration with the poignant line: "I never married."

When I reached my office, I got out my script, studied the sequences once more, and suddenly realized why Zanuck had cut them, with or without Ford's acquiescence. Though all of them chronicled important advances in the development of the adolescent boy's character, none of them advanced the story itself. Darryl had merely done what he always did: cut to the bone of the story line.

There's an amusing postscript to this Case of the Missing Sequences. Jim Pepper, when we first discussed this book, had indicated the cut sequences in a copy of the script. I showed the scenes to Roddy McDowall, and received a stunning surprise: he had no recollection of ever having played them. In fact, he joked that they were so wonderful that he ought to call Twentieth Century-Fox and demand the right to play them now.

But to me this revelation was no joke. If the scenes had been cut before they could be shot, then Zanuck and Ford had conspired—the word popped into my mind—to chop up my script without consulting me. Suddenly I found myself, after fifty years, with my anger, first kindled by what I had considered a misguided retake, now for another reason once again aflame. I felt deeply hurt that my two old friends, Darryl and Jack, could have been guilty of such perfidy. This after half a century, and years since they both had gone to their rewards.

Fortunately, Jim Pepper rescued me from more of such foolishness. From his research files, he produced stills of all the scenes that had been cut, proof positive that they had been shot. It was Roddy's memory that was at fault. There had been no producer-director conspiracy, no ganging up on the poor writer. The scenes had been shot and had become victims, for better or worse, of customary editing procedures.

This is not the place to summarize in detail the successes of *How Green Was My Valley*, with the critics (most of them), the public (hordes of them), and in the hindsight of cinematic historians. It was nominated for ten Academy Awards and won five, including Best Director and Best Picture, this in the year of *Citizen Kane*. It won for Ford the much-prized New York Film Critics Award, his fourth.

How did it fare in Wales itself? I have heard that there was some criticism because our approach was too sentimental, the 1941 British *The Stars Look Down* being deemed more realistic. I had one direct report when I was shooting on location in Wales in 1961, from the manager of the Swansea theater where, after the last show, we ran our rushes every night. After he had told me that his current offering was a flop, pointing to that evening's meagre litter of paper, chewing-gum and cigarette butts, I asked him how *How Green Was My Valley* had done. He said that it was extremely popular, but that he suffered from a poor turnover. People would come in for the early show, join with the singers on the screen in belting out the old Welsh songs, and then stay for a second and even a third show to do it all over again. Apparently we had invented a new way for a movie to lose money.

As we prepared this book, Jack's fourth New York Critics Award belatedly handed me another surprise—or perhaps shock would be a better word.

During World War II, I was in charge of production for Robert Riskin's Motion Picture Bureau of the Office of War Information, Overseas Branch, a cumbersome title for our mission, which was to make propaganda films for distribution overseas. My job necessitated a weekly trip from our headquarters in New York to Washington. I always tried to drop in on Commander Ford in his Navy Department office when he wasn't off to some more exciting locale, such as Midway Island, where he covered on film that island's gallant defense in *The Battle of Midway*.

Parenthetically, not many Hollywood people in war service actually came under fire, like Willy Wyler and Jack Ford. We were set to doing what we knew best, which was to make movies. I should cite another exception in Colonel Darryl Zanuck, who, when I ran into him in Washington, opened the conversation by asking me if I had ever had dysentery under fire. I was forced to answer feebly that my most harrowing wartime experience had been post-nasal drip under the Third Avenue Elevated.

In the spring of 1942, I saw on Ford's Navy Department desk his award from the New York critics. I congratulated him on winning it as well as the Oscar, adding rather churlishly that I wished I had gotten more out of the picture than just my salary. As a matter of fact, I had been so busy that I hadn't paid much attention to the Academy Awards, not even discovering that I had been nominated until my certificate arrived in the mail. In those days, Oscar didn't receive the worldwide attention he does today.

Ford pounced on my surly remark: "You greedy bastard, you won the Academy. What more do you want?" When I told him that I hadn't won, he waved it away by saying that probably a lot of goddam Republicans had voted against me, and that I could win it next year, or the year after. (As a matter of fact, being young and inexperienced, I was equally confident that I could do just that.) We went out to drink consternation to Hitler, Tojo, and all Republican members of the Academy.

The next day, the award, inscribed in red crayon: "Thanks Phil—Affection Jack," arrived at my office in New York. At the time, I was embarrassed that my stupid remark had been so magnificently rewarded. I regretted ever having made it, and, a few weeks later when we met in New York, Amanda and I begged him to take back his award, but he wouldn't hear of it. So I hung it on the wall of my study.

I remained embarrassed for fifty years, until Jim Pepper said one day that he had on his wall all of Jack's original New York Film Critics Awards, including that one. After some disputation over the phone, he sent me a color photograph of his version. The key word in that sentence is "color." Jim's award—the real one, of course—is in beautiful color. Mine—the photographic copy I had seen on Jack's desk—is in drab black and white, which fails to do justice to the artistry of its designer.

This story is quintessential John Ford. That addict of practical jokes, that labyrinthine Irish con man, couldn't resist the gargantuan jest of letting me go on thinking that he had given me his original award, instead of one of possibly several copies. I am now speculating on when he became aware of the fact that I thought I had the original. Perhaps right away in his office, but I think it more likely that he had his first inkling of it when Amanda and I pleaded with him to take it back. Perhaps he intended to enlighten me later on, and then forgot all about it.

I should add that it still hangs in the place of honor in my study.

The more I ponder on the character of Jack Ford, the more surprises come to light. In politics, he is usually considered a right-winger, possibly a case of guilt by association with his favorite satellites, John Wayne and Ward Bond. In fact, in 1937, he and Melvyn Douglas and I, representing the three major crafts, were officers of the Motion Picture Democratic Committee, militantly anti-Nazi and pro-New Deal, and later called by some a communist front, because in those innocent days before the Nazi-Soviet pact of 1939, communists, calling themselves "progressives," were active in all such organizations. At the time Jack called himself "always left—definitely a socialist democrat" (probably a Fordian exaggeration), actively supported the Spanish Loyalists against the fascists, and, fifteen years later, while taking pride in his naval rank of admiral, helped forestall an attempt by Cecil B. DeMille to involve the Directors Guild in blacklisting its own members.

In other ways, he was similarly complicated. He has been accused of cruelty bordering on sadism, especially to his actors, with many accounts of how he enjoyed reducing such he-men as Wayne and Victor McLaglen to blubbering incoherence on the set. Yet Roddy McDowall always describes him in such words as "kind—gentle—dear." He gives Jack full credit for coaxing out of him that memorable performance. Anna Lee was afraid that Ford would replace her because she was English. On the contrary, they became lifelong friends. He always treated her with the greatest consideration, with the slight obeisance to his Irish heritage of calling her "Limey." Perhaps the truth is that, like Zanuck, he delighted in pushing over only those intended by nature to be pushovers.

As to what happened on the set, I have to rely on the people who were there. They are unanimous in describing it as a happy ship, likening it also to a harmonious and loving family. All give full credit to Ford. And this warm glow has persisted over the years. The movie is still alive in the minds of the survivors; friendships made then still endure. Maureen O'Hara and Anna Lee still call themselves "women of the green valley," and Maureen named her daughter "Bronwyn," after Anna's character (with a slight difference in the spelling).

And this brings me to the greatest Ford surprise of all. Anna reports that he told her that this was his favorite among all his movies, even though it was not a canonical Ford epic such as *Stagecoach* or *The Informer*, but more like *Young Mr. Lincoln* and *The Grapes of Wrath*, a product of Zanuck's assembly line. I would find Anna's report hard to believe were there not other indications that it could well be true. He usually shunned awards ceremonies, but he made it a point to accept in person the award of the New York critics, though he had done this for none of his other winners, nor for his four Academy Awards. In October 1972, the Directors Guild, aware that Jack's illness was terminal, honored him with an evening. They asked him to choose which movie to show; out of them all, he picked *How Green Was My Valley*.

The Guild theater was packed that night; old directors, a few of them in wheel-chairs, young ones in their beads, beards and levis. Of our cast, Roddy, Maureen, Anna and Walter Pidgeon were able to come.

It was at once a sad occasion and a triumph, a fitting period to a great artist's life. There were two huge ovations: when the end title came on, and when Jack was helped on to the stage. Then those of us who had participated trooped up, one by one, to lesser ovations, to offer our tributes. As I came over to shake his hand he glared at me and asked: "Where's Amanda?" I pointed her out in the audience, whereupon this Lord Nelson of the sound stages, with his black eye-patch and his quarterdeck voice, straightened in his chair and barked: "Come on up here!" She too received an ovation, though I'm sure that nobody knew who she was.

Then we adjourned to the Guild's board room for a private celebration. There were drinks, a little song and much laughter, before our old friend was helped out to his car. Then there were tears.

What Richard Llewellyn wrote is true: "For there is no fence nor hedge round Time that is gone. You can go back and have what you like of it—if you can remember." In writing these notes, I have been wallowing quite shamelessly in memory, in this unexpected attempt on my part to recapture *temps perdu*.

But perhaps Proust is wrong and Llewellyn right: nothing is really lost. After fifty years, it is all still very much alive to me. Only a movie, but also a catalyst to revive old friendships and old friends, old times and places. Only a movie? Perhaps. Sentimentalism? Perhaps. But I think again of what Roddy McDowall had to say of that particular time and place: "The happiest place to make movies in all the world."

And so indeed it was: the triumphs and disasters, the good reviews and bad, the hit movies and the stinkers, the harmonious collaborations and the bitter quarrels, this year's "greatest picture ever made" withering under the cold eyes of some preview audience in San Diego, while in San Bernardino, Virginia Zanuck comes breathlessly out into the draughty forecourt of the theater to inform us: "They love it in the ladies' room!"

Memories. How green was Darryl's office!

20TH CENTURY-FOX FILM CORPORATION
PRESENTS

HOW GREEN WAS MY VALLEY

Produced by DARRYL F. ZANUCK

Directed by JOHN FORD

Screenplay by PHILIP DUNNE

Based on the Novel by RICHARD LLEWELLYN

Cinematographer: ARTHUR MILLER

Music: ALFRED NEWMAN

Choral Effects by EISTEDDFOD SINGERS OF WALES

Editor: JAMES B. CLARK

Narrator: IRVING PICHEL

Narrator for United Kingdom Version: RHYS WILLIAMS

Art Direction: RICHARD DAY and NATHAN JURAN

Make-Up: GUY PIERCE

Set Decorator: THOMAS LITTLE

Costumes: GWEN WAKELING

Sound: EUGENE GROSSMAN and ROGER HEMAN

Filmed in Black & White

Running Time: 118 Minutes

THE CAST

MR. GRUFFYDD	WALTER PIDGEON
ANGHARAD MORGAN	MAUREEN O'HARA
GWILYM MORGAN	DONALD CRISP
MRS. BETH MORGAN	SARA ALLGOOD
BRONWEN MORGAN	ANNA LEE
HUW MORGAN	RODDY McDOWALL
IANTO MORGAN	JOHN LODER
IVOR MORGAN	PATRICK KNOWLES
DAVY MORGAN	RICHARD FRASER
OWEN MORGAN	JAMES MONKS
YOUNG GWILYM MORGAN	EVAN S. EVANS
DAI BANDO	RHYS WILLIAMS
CYFARTHA	BARRY FITZGERALD
THE WELSH SINGERS	THEMSELVES
MR. JONAS	MORTON LOWERY
MR. PARRY	ARTHUR SHIELDS
CEINWEN	ANN TODD
DR. RICHARDS	FREDERIC WORLOCK
OLD EVANS	LIONEL PAPE
MRS. NICHOLAS	ETHEL GRIFFIES
IESTYN EVANS	MARTEN LAMONT
MEILLYN LEWIS	EVE MARCH
MINER'S WIFE	MAE MARSH
MINER	LOUIS JEAN HEYDT
ENSEMBLE SINGER	TUDOR WILLIAMS
POSTMAN	HERBERT EVANS
EVE	MARY FIELD
BIT WOMAN	MARY GORDON
SHOP KEEPER	TINY JONES
MERVYN	CLIFFORD SEVERN
Additionally	FRANK BAKER
TAILOR (cut from final release)	JOSEPH M. KERRIGAN
MOTSHILL (cut from final release)	DENIS HOEY

How Green Was My Valley won Academy Awards for Best Picture (Darryl F. Zanuck), Best Director (John Ford), Best Supporting Actor (Donald Crisp), Best Cinematography (Arthur Miller), Best Art Direction (Richard Day, Nathan Juran combined with set decorator Thomas Little). Additionally, the film was nominated for Academy Awards for Best Screenplay (Philip Dunne), Best Supporting Actress (Sara Allgood), Best Editing (James B. Clark), Best Musical Score (Alfred Newman), Best Sound (Eugene Crossman and Roger Heman).

The New York Film Critics presented John Ford their Best Direction Award of 1941.

38

John Ford, Roddy McDowall, and Philip Dunne on the set of
How Green Was My Valley.

40   Filming on the Welsh village set in the Malibu hills.

The Morgan Family.

41

Above & below: Deleted scene of Huw helping Gruffydd to make the frame for the
Queen Victoria portrait presented to Ivor Morgan.

42

Deleted woodworking scene.

Deleted scene of Huw and Gruffydd repairing the pencil box.   43

Deleted scene of Huw being measured for long pants.

Deleted scene of Huw and Matt Harries, Bronwen's suitor.

Above & below: Deleted scene of Ianto Morgan knocking down Iestyn Evans for daring to speak to Angharad as originally scripted by Philip Dunne.

Deleted scene of Huw and Ceinwen.

46   The impending departure of sons young Gwilym and Owen Morgan.

Darryl and Virginia Zanuck.

48

HOW GREEN WAS
MY VALLEY

Screenplay by Philip Dunne

HOW GREEN WAS MY VALLEY

PART ONE

We hear a magnificent choir of men's voices singing one of the great Welsh songs. The voices continue through the opening scene, but more softly when the voice of the Narrator comes in.

We see HUW's HANDS, the hands of a man about sixty, carefully folding some shirts, ties and socks into an old blue cloth. As the hands knot the blue cloth round the clothes, the scene shifts to the window, so that we can see, beyond, a typical WELSH COAL VALLEY, ugly, dirty, dominated by its stacks, cranes and towering slag heap. Not far from the window the great slag heap rises in a broken sweep, high into the sky.

HUW'S VOICE (*simultaneous with the unfolding scenes*). *I am packing my belongings in the little blue cloth my mother used to tie around her hair when she did the house, and I am going from my Valley. And this time I shall never return.*

I am leaving behind me my sixty years of memory— Memory.

There is strange that the mind will forget so much of what only this moment is passed, and yet hold so clear and bright the memory of what happened years ago —of men and women long since dead. For there is no fence nor hedge round Time that is gone. You can go back and have what you like of it—if you can remember.

The scene shifts, as if passing through the window, until we are looking up the steep STREET. In the background are the slag heap and the collieries. Moving up and down the street are poorly dressed men, walking bent because of the steepness of the street. The houses are built of quarry stone, grimy and huddled together—an atmosphere of poverty and decay. Finally the entire ugly coal VALLEY spreads before us. Smoke, blackness, poverty.

Then the picture dims slowly down as the Valley, as it once was, appears, fresh and green, each detail in the new scene fitting in with its counterpart in the old. The Chapel, almost hidden in the first scene, now stands bravely in view. Next we see the COLLIERY with only a small slag heap—a splotch of ugly black on the green; then, the CHAPEL dominating the street.

And now we see the COLLIERY with only a small slag heap—a splotch of ugly black on the green.

The Exterior of the CHAPEL is next seen, dominating the street.

HUW'S VOICE. *So I can close my eyes on my Valley as it is today—and it is gone— and I see it as it was when I was a boy. Green it was, and possessed of the plenty of the earth. In all Wales, there was none so beautiful, for the colliery had only begun to poke its skinny black fingers through the green. The black slag— the waste of the coalpits—made only a small pile then—and our little Chapel was master of the Valley from where it stood at the head of the street.*

Far down below a man and boy appear, slowly climbing the hill. They are GWILYM MORGAN and his ten-year-old son, the same HUW who is the Narrator of our picture. Both wear the clothes of the period around 1890. They are of a family of coal miners and are attired accordingly. Morgan is smiling down at Huw as the boy struggles to keep up with his father's great strides.

HUW is seen drinking in what his father says. He looks round him as if expecting actually to see the men of whom his father is speaking. Then the two stop on the ridge of the hill, where they are silhouetted against the golden light that bathes the Valley. The wind blows through their hair.

HUW'S VOICE. *Everything I ever learnt as a small boy came from my father, and I never found anything he ever told me to be wrong or worthless. He used to tell me of my Valley and its people—the brave men of Wales who never bowed to Roman or Danish or Saxon conquerors until so many had died that the women could not bear enough children to fill the ranks. The Men of the Valley, long since gathered to their Fathers—became as real to me as if I had met them face to face. But the battles they had fought had been long forgotten and we of my Valley fought a new fight now—to wrest from beneath the green the black wealth of Nature: the coal—which first enriched us and then made us poorer than we had been before. Coal miners were my father and all my brothers—and proud of our trade as our ancestors had been of theirs.*

The scene dissolves, first to the COLLIERY WHISTLE, which is blowing, and then to a section of the colliery, a COLLIERY CUTTING, with IVOR, the eldest of the Morgan sons, punching at the coal face with his pick. He wears a miner's outfit and is blackened and grimy with the coal dust.

HUW'S VOICE. *We were a big family. After my father: Ivor, the eldest—solid and dependable as the mountainside.*

In ANOTHER CUTTING, IANTO, second of the sons, up to his waist in water, is levering out a boulder with a crowbar. Ianto turns at the sound of the whistle.

HUW'S VOICE. *Ianto—who had the devil's own tongue and liked a fight better than the blood in his veins—*

DAVY is seen, pick on shoulder, lantern in hand. He is coming down from one of the cuttings.

HUW'S VOICE. *Davy, the brain of the family—*

OWEN AND GWILYM appear trundling a barrowful of coal.

HUW'S VOICE. *Owen, the dreamer, whom we seldom heard speak—Gwilym, who was named for my father, and yet as quick with his tongue as my father was slow—*

The scene dissolves to the interior of the COLLIERY, where the miners, with Morgan and his sons prominent, are taking their places in the CAGE. It moves slowly up, revealing some adolescent boys.

At the MINE ENTRANCE. It is day, and the stalwart miners, grimy with coal dust, are coming from the cages and lining up to get their pay. The Morgans again are prominent.

IVOR is seen receiving his pay in gold from the paymaster in his little booth. There are gold coins on the paymaster's counter. Ivor drops one and it rings faintly.

HUW'S VOICE. *Saturday was the great day, for then the men would be paid off as they came off the morning shift.*

In those early days of the colliery, money was easily earned, and plenty of it. And not in pieces of paper, either. Solid gold sovereigns, yellow as summer daffodils—and they rang when you hit them on something solid.

We see the MORGAN HOUSE, where ANGHARAD, a pretty girl of seventeen, stands in the door looking up toward the colliery. She goes into the house and reappears with a stool which she sets outside the door. After a moment, MRS. MORGAN (BETH) comes out, wearing a snowy white apron, and sits on the stool, spreading the apron.

At the COLLIERY the miners start down the hill in a solid, compact mass. As they approach, one of them, in the foreground, opens his mouth and starts a song. Others immediately join in the rich Welsh harmony.

And now we can see the miners marching DOWN THE HILL, still singing. As they pass each house, a little group breaks off and goes to the house. Morgan and his five grown sons leave the procession and turn in at the little gate of the MORGAN HOUSE. Morgan throws his sovereigns in his wife's lap and passes into the house. IVOR passes next with a smile for his mother, the other brothers following. IANTO tweaks Huw's ear as he passes.

HUW'S VOICE. *My sister Angharad would warn my mother that the men were coming up the hill. On pay day, all the women would dress up specially in their second best, with starched stiff aprons. One of the men would strike up a song.*

54

Singing is in my people as sight is in the eye.

As the men came up they threw their wages, sovereign by sovereign, into the shining laps, fathers first, sons and lodgers in a line behind. With my father and five brothers working we had forty every week for the box on our mantelpiece.

The scene dissolves to the INTERIOR OF THE MORGAN SHED. The boys have stripped to the waist and are having the grime scrubbed off their backs by their sister and Huw. Buckets of water and towels are in evidence. A pair of GRIMY HANDS is seen. Their owner scrubs at them without avail, leaving the black lines of coal dust.

The boys towel themselves vigorously, with Huw standing on tiptoe to reach Ivor's broad shoulders. HUW looks with distaste at his own lily-white hands.

HUW'S VOICE. *Then the scrubbing—out in the shed. My mother had drawn the buckets of hot water and cold and I used to help my sister scrub the coal dust from my brothers' backs. Most would come off them, but the hands were hopeless. Scrub and scrub, Mr. Coal would lie there and laugh at you. It is the honorable badge of the coal miner and I envied it on my grown-up brothers.*

The scene dissolves to the INTERIOR OF THE MORGAN KITCHEN, where Morgan is seated at the head of his table. His head is raised as his lips move in the act of saying grace. All are standing. We see the bountifully laden table and the expectant family waiting. Huw squirms restlessly, and his father shoots him a look.

Morgan is carving and Beth is ladling out soup for the family. The plates are passed round and the family begins to eat.

HUW'S VOICE. *Then dinner, with my father saying the grace, looking up at the stain in the ceiling, and maybe giving me a look under his brows if I moved. There was always a baron of beef and a shoulder or leg of lamb at my father's elbow. And chickens or ducks or goose—and plenty of vegetables—and the soup. There was a smell with that soup—vital with herbs fresh from the untroubled ground. If happiness has a smell, I know*

it well—for in those days it was all over our house.

There was never any talk while we were eating. I never met anybody whose talk was better than good food.

Beth moves to the stove to lift a lid off a pot. She looks back at her family, smiling.

HUW'S VOICE. *My mother was always on the run—always the last to start her dinner and the first to finish. For, if my father was the head of our house, my mother was its heart.*

The scene dissolves to ANGHARAD washing dishes in the sink. Huw stands with a towel, wiping.

HUW'S VOICE. *After dinner, when dishes had been washed, the box was brought to the table, for the spending money to be handed out.*

We see the INTERIOR OF THE PARLOR, the box on the mantelpiece. Beth lifts down the box, takes it over to the table, and sets it down in front of her husband, who is smoking his pipe. The sons are gathered round. As Morgan opens the box, Huw and Angharad hurry in from the kitchen. Morgan begins to hand out small amounts of money to his children as they step up in order of their age, but first he gives some to Beth, and with it an affectionate kiss.

HUW'S VOICE. *My father used to say that money was made to be spent just as men spend their strength and brains in earning it—and as willingly—but always with a purpose.*

HUW, as the youngest, is last in line. He stands eagerly and expectantly. Morgan gives him a playful frown and then puts a penny in his hand. As soon as he gets the penny, Huw turns and runs from the room like one possessed. Morgan and Beth laugh after him.

Huw reaches the door. He starts out, then stops, hurries back and grabs his cap and runs out once more.

Huw darts out of the house. Then he runs up the street and around a corner.

HUW'S VOICE. *I had my Saturday penny every week.—Out of the house and round the corner—as I had run a hundred times before.*

Huw appears, still running, at the LITTLE GREEN IN FRONT OF THE CHAPEL. He slows down to a respectful walk as he approaches the Chapel, and walks past it, touching his cap politely to a dignified elderly couple.

HUW'S VOICE. *Softly now, for respect for Chapel was the first thing my father taught us.*

As soon as he passed, he breaks into a run once more, reaching A SMALL SIDE STREET, where he runs up to a small bakery and confectionery shop, embellished with a sign:

TOSSALL
BAKERY AND CONFECTIONS

and darts in. A bell jingles from somewhere within the shop. Soon Huw is dancing impatiently from foot to foot before the counter. A benign, elderly woman hands him a package of toffee, which she has all ready for him, and accepts his penny. Huw gives her a polite little bow and turns to leave the shop. He goes out the door, the bell jingling once more. He is cramming the toffee into his mouth and is in heaven. He chews mightily and stuffs in some more. Some of it gets caught round a back tooth and he puts in an exploring finger to straighten it out.

HUW'S VOICE. *Then straight to Mrs. Tossall, the Shop for that toffee which you could chew for hours, it seems to me now, and even after it had gone down, you could swallow and still find the taste of it hiding behind your tongue. It is with me now—so many years later. It makes me think of so much that was good that is gone.*

It was on this afternoon that I first saw Bron—Bronwen— She had come over from the next valley for her first call on my mother—

HUW comes back to his own house. He stops near the gate, looking off down the street. The chewing motion of his jaws slows.

Approaching the gate, walking up the steep hill, is a very pretty girl with a double basket held on her hip, her hat tied under her chin with a gay bit of ribbon.

As BRONWEN approaches the gate we begin to hear her footsteps, the Chapel bell tolling, the rumble of wagon wheels, all the dim murmuring sounds of a little village come to life. Bronwen looks inquiringly at the house, turns in at the gate, which creaks, and stops as she sees Huw. She smiles.

BRONWEN. Is this Gwilym Morgan's house?

Huw, staring at her, nods.

BRONWEN (*smiling*). You must be Huw.

Huw gulps, turns and darts into the house. Bronwen laughs as she moves towards it.

Beth is at the table under the window in the MORGAN KITCHEN, cutting a pie. Huw runs excitedly in.

BETH. What's the matter with you?

Huw cannot speak; he points, gaping, into the parlor.

BETH (*looking up*). Oh—

She puts down her knife, straightens her hair hurriedly, and seeing Bronwen standing outside the door of the PARLOR, goes to meet her.

BETH. Is that you, Bronwen?

BRONWEN (*whispering*). Yes.

BETH. Come in, my child.

She opens the door; Bronwen comes in. Beth kisses her in warm greeting, then stands back to look at her.

BETH. There is lovely you are. I am so proud for Ivor.

BRONWEN (*shyly*). I'm the one to be proud.

BETH (*laughing*). You think well of our Ivor? It seems only a few months since he was scratching round like this one here (*indicating Huw, who is still gaping*) with his mouth open.

She puts a finger under his chin to close his mouth, then takes Bronwen's basket and gives it to Huw.

BETH (*to Huw*). This is Bronwen, Huw, who is to be your sister.

BRONWEN (*with a smile*). We've already met.

She bends down to kiss Huw, who reacts to this with wonder and awe, touching his finger to his cheek.

BRONWEN (*smiling*). Be careful of the basket. There's shortcake in it.

It is less a warning than an invitation to help himself. But Huw's mind is not on shortcake. Then Morgan's voice is heard.

MORGAN'S VOICE (*heartily*). Well—

Morgan comes down the stairs, followed by his sons. He smiles at Bronwen, then crooks a finger over his shoulder.

MORGAN. Ivor—

Ivor comes down the stairs, looking at Bronwen. The brothers grin at him covertly. Morgan, grinning, pushes Ivor toward Bronwen. As Ivor is about to take Bronwen in his arms, Morgan, who has observed Huw gaping, takes him by the back of the neck and leads him toward the stairway. Huw would like to look back, but doesn't dare.

MORGAN (*grinning*). Those things are not for you, my son. You will have your turn to come.

He gives Huw a friendly push up the stairs and goes back into the room.

HUW is seen reluctantly climbing the stairs, stopping occasionally to look wistfully back. He can hear the happy, excited voices of the people below: Ivor's brothers meeting Bronwen, congratulating Ivor.

HUW'S VOICE. *I think I fell in love with Bronwen then. Perhaps it is silly to think a child could fall in love. But I am the child that was, and nobody knows how I felt, except only me. And I think I fell in love with Bronwen that Saturday on the hill.*

The scene dissolves to the EXTERIOR OF THE CHAPEL. It is day. Crowds of people, all dressed in their best, are entering. This dissolves to the INTERIOR, which is packed, men sitting on one side, women on the other.

IVOR is waiting nervously with Ianto beside him and his other brothers behind him.

Bronwen, in her wedding dress, is seen coming up the aisle on her father's arm.

Beth and Bronwen's mother are crying happily into their handkerchiefs. Morgan and Bronwen's father, as the latter steps back from Bronwen to stand beside Morgan, are both perspiring and uncomfortable. The Morgan brothers, with Huw, are standing solemnly.

MERDDYN GRUFFYDD, the minister, is standing at the head of the aisle as Ivor and Bronwen take their places before him. He looks at them with his head on one side, smiling a little, and with something of appraisal in his eyes. They shift a little uneasily.

HUW'S VOICE. *All our Valley came to the wedding, and Bron's valley, too—and Chapel packed so full you could not raise your elbows.*

Ivor had my father's white waistcoat and there is a swell he was with the pinks in his buttonhole. And Bron in her great-grandmother's wedding dress.

My mother and Bron's were crying down in front, and her father and mine looking unhappy in their high collars and top hats. And all my brothers as solemn as a funeral. But the new preacher—Mr. Gruffydd—was not solemn. It was my first sight of him. I remember how he smiled—and looked at Ivor and Bronwen —and waited—and waited—almost as if he would refuse to marry them unless he could learn right there from looking at them that they would be happy together.

The congregation is waiting for the minister to begin the services, some of the elders in the front pews rather startled by Gruffydd's easy informality. GRUFFYDD is still smiling down at Ivor and Bronwen. Then his eyes grow serious and he begins the ceremony.

The scene dissolves to the CHAPEL GREEN. Long tables, loaded with food, have been set up before the Chapel. The happy wedding guests are thronged round the tables, laughing and chatting. Prominent is an enormous wedding cake.

The scene dissolves to the EXTERIOR OF THE MORGAN HOUSE, at night. Celebrants are waiting round with tankards as Morgan swings a bung-starter on a barrel of beer. The beer gushes forth. Morgan begins to fill the tankards, straightening to take an enormous gulp himself. Beth, inside the house, is dispensing tea to the women.

> HUW's VOICE. *I will never forget the party after the wedding—and the wedding cake it took two men to lift.*
>
> *It was one of the few times I ever saw my father drink too much beer—but if a man cannot get drunk on the night his eldest son marries and gives him a chance for grandchildren, let us all go into the earth and be quick about it. Everyone was drunk that night, and if tea had been beer, the women would have been on the floor, too.*

Next we see the GUESTS assembled, singing. Ivor, now in his ordinary Sunday best, is leading them. The MORGAN FAMILY is sitting with others on the porch, Huw sitting with Mr. Gruffydd and his father and mother, all singing. A short distance away, Angharad sits with Ianto, Davy, Owen, and Gwilym. They, too, are singing. Huw looks up at Gruffydd, who is singing with vigor and enthusiasm and GRUFFYDD continuing to sing, gives Huw a little smile. Angharad, seen among her brothers, looks over toward Gruffydd and stops singing as she watches him.

HUW notices that Angharad is not singing. He follows her glance to Gruffydd, looks back at her, then back at Gruffydd, as if he understands the reason for her silence. Gruffydd is oblivious of Angharad's adoring gaze.

> HUW's VOICE. *We made a noise to lift the mountain from its base, indeed, and we learned Mr. Gruffydd could sing as well as he could preach. And Angharad could not sing at all for watching him.*

We see ANGHARAD, IANTO and DAVY—Angharad still looking at Gruffydd. Ianto notices that she is silent and gives her a hearty nudge in the ribs. Angharad hastily begins to sing once more.

The crowd is singing under the stars, with lighted windows of the houses round them.

> HUW's VOICE. *And round about us the Valley echoed with the happy voices—*

happy, then—all of us—but soon there was to be trouble.

The scene dissolves to the MINE ENTRANCE by day. A mine employee is tacking up a card, headed:

WAGE SCHEDULE
EFFECTIVE AUGUST 3RD

The men gather round. An angry buzz goes up from them. A bitter voice rises.

> MINER. Up to our waists in water all week—and paid short today.

Morgan and his sons, along with several other miners, shoulder their way into the forefront of the scene, and read the notice, frowning. Morgan looks up thoughtfully at the mine office.

OUTSIDE THE MINE OFFICE, Christmas Evans, the owner, stands with his manager. They go back into the office. Morgan turns to Ivor, who is beside him.

> MORGAN. Ivor—find Dai Griffiths and Idris John and bring them to the office.

Ivor leaves. Morgan turns to go but Ianto detains him.

> IANTO. Will we come with you?
>
> MORGAN. No. This is a matter for the older men. Home to your mother and ask her to keep my supper hot.

Davy frowns as Morgan leaves.

> DAVY. But—

Ianto puts his hand on Davy's arm, restraining him.

> IANTO. Leave it now, Davy.

Both look off after their father with worried frowns.

The scene dissolves to the MORGAN PARLOR. The Morgan boys are sitting tensely, waiting. Beth can be seen in her kitchen in the background, Huw and Angharad helping her. Morgan comes quietly in, and crosses to hang up his jacket. His back is to the boys, but we can see his face. He looks angry and bitter. He pauses without turning as he hangs his coat.

> MORGAN (*quietly*). Why aren't you washed?

IANTO. We were waiting for you.

Morgan turns as Beth comes in. Morgan speaks to her kindly.

MORGAN. The cut is only a few shillings. There will still be plenty for all of us. (*Patting her arm*) A bit of supper now, is it, girl?

Beth goes back into the kitchen. Morgan turns to the boys, who are still eyeing him steadily. He is taking his time over satisfying their curiosity. Finally, he speaks:

MORGAN. It is because they are not getting the old price for coal. Come and wash, now.

He starts to go, but Ianto stops him.

IANTO. May we speak, first?

MORGAN. Yes.

IANTO. They have not given you the real reason for this cut.

Morgan's eyebrows go up.

DAVY (*nodding*). We have been expecting it for weeks—ever since the iron works at Dowlais closed down.

MORGAN. What have the iron works to do with us?

IANTO. The men from Dowlais have come to the colliery, willing to work for any wage—so all our wages must come down.

Davy, standing near the box on the mantelpiece, nods gloomily.

DAVY. And this is only a beginning. Watch, now. They will cut us again and still again, until they have this—(*tapping the box*)—as empty as their promises.

MORGAN. Nonsense. A good worker is worth good wages, and he will get them.

IANTO. Not while there are three men for every job.

DAVY (*pressing the point*). Why should the owners pay more—if men are willing to work for less?

MORGAN. Because they are not savages! They are men, too. Like us.

IANTO (*quietly*). Men, yes. But not like us. Would they deal with you just now when you went to them?

MORGAN (*honestly*). No.

IANTO. That's because they have power and we have none.

MORGAN (*with irony*). How will we get power, then? From the air?

The boys exchange another look, then Davy speaks with deliberation.

DAVY. No—from a union of all the men.

Morgan's lips compress.

MORGAN. Union, is it? (*With studied distaste*) I had no thought I would ever hear my own sons talking socialist nonsense.

DAVY (*hotly*). But it's sense. Good sense. Unless we stand together—

MORGAN (*cutting in*). I have had enough of this talk.

DAVY (*protesting*). But, Father—

Morgan turns his gaze full on him, looking him in the eyes. Davy stares for a moment, then subsides. Morgan, having established his mastery over his sons, returns to his normal tone.

MORGAN. Come and wash, now. Your good mother will be waiting.

Morgan leads the way out, Huw watching with wide eyes, sensing the bad feeling that exists between father and sons.

The scene dissolves to the EXTERIOR OF THE COLLIERY. A rainy day. Huw is going home from school, carrying books. He stops short as he comes to the colliery entrance, looking up to where the checkers are checking the trams loaded with coal that the men push past them. Two of the checkers stand under little sheds. Morgan, the third, is standing in the pouring rain without a shed. Huw stares at his father.

Morgan is grim-faced as he does his job in the pouring rain. Ianto and Davy approach with their trams. They are looking accusingly at their father, who averts his eyes from them. He looks over the coal in their trams, makes a check mark and waves them past. They hesitate a moment, then they go on past. Morgan turns to check a tram pushed by another miner as the scene dissolves to:

The INTERIOR OF THE MORGAN HOUSE. The family is at dinner. They are silent and tense, the boys looking at their father out of the corners of their eyes. He is eating quietly. Davy suddenly jumps to his feet, shaking his fist.

> DAVY (*with sudden anger*). Do you think I will let them make my father stand like a dog in the rain and not raise my hands to stop it?
>
> BETH (*scandalized*). Hisht, Davy—

All turn to look at Morgan, who finishes chewing what is in his mouth and then turns to look at Davy.

> MORGAN (*quietly*). Who gave you permission to speak?
>
> DAVY (*stubbornly*). This matter is too important for silence. They're trying to punish you—
>
> MORGAN (*cutting in*). It is not more important than good manners.
>
> DAVY (*heatedly*). But what are we going to do about it? You will die of the cold when it comes to snow.
>
> IANTO (*nodding grimly*). Let us all stand together and see how they will act, then.
>
> DAVY. Right. The men will come out if we say the word. All the pits are ready.

At this, Morgan's eyes harden. He speaks with quiet deliberation and emphasis.

> MORGAN. You will not make me a plank for your politics. I will not be the excuse for any strike.
>
> IANTO. But if they learn they can do things like that to the spokesman, what will they try and do to the men?
>
> MORGAN. We will see. Be silent, now, and finish your supper.
>
> DAVY (*desperately*). But—Father—
>
> MORGAN (*sharply*). Enough, now.

His manner says plainly that he will tolerate no more of this talk. He begins to eat his dinner. Davy sits down, but Owen slams down his fork.

> OWEN. It is not enough!
>
> MORGAN (*sternly*). Owen—
>
> OWEN (*doggedly*). I am sorry, sir—but—
>
> MORGAN (*quietly*). Hold your tongue at table until you have permission to speak.
>
> OWEN. I will speak against injustice anywhere—with permission or without it.
>
> MORGAN. Not in this house.
>
> OWEN. In this house and outside.
>
> MORGAN (*quietly*). Leave the table.
>
> OWEN (*also quietly*). I will leave the house.

He pushes back his chair and rises. Beth puts out her hand to her husband.

> BETH. Gwil— (*To Owen.*) Tell your father you're sorry.
>
> OWEN (*stubbornly*). I'm not sorry.

Gwilym suddenly springs to his feet.

> GWILYM. I'm with you! We can find lodgings in the village.
>
> BETH (*shocked*). Gwilym!

Morgan sits like a rock, his eyes traveling slowly to his other sons. It is a challenge to them to choose sides and state their intentions. Davy meets his look defiantly, then slowly rises to his feet. Morgan's look passes over to Ianto. Reluctantly, Ianto joins the others.

> MORGAN. All of you, then?

They nod silently, in unison.

> MORGAN (*quietly*). You have one more chance. Sit down—finish your dinner—and I will say no more.
>
> IANTO (*also quietly*). We are not questioning your authority, sir, but if manners prevent our speaking the truth—we will be without manners.

There is a moment's pause, then Morgan picks up his knife and fork.

> MORGAN. Get your clothes and go.

The four boys turn and go slowly toward the stairs, Huw watching breathlessly. Morgan resumes his dinner, outwardly

60

calm, but his hand trembles slightly as it carries his fork to his mouth.

BETH. Oh, Gwilym— (*She begins to sob quietly.*)

Angharad rises and begins to stack the plates. She looks at her father, and then her mother, then puts down the plates.

ANGHARAD (*mutinously*). I'm going with them—to look after them.

Beth whirls on her, her tears forgotten. In her emotion, she slaps Angharad lightly.

BETH. Close your mouth, girl. Get on with your dishes.

She means what she says. Angharad wilts, picks up the plates and goes to the sink. Beth looks up toward the stairs.

In the UPSTAIRS BEDROOM, used by all the boys, with five beds in it, Ianto, Davy, Owen, and Gwilym are packing their clothes in bundles, rolling up their mattresses.

In the KITCHEN Beth turns and goes slowly to the sink after Angharad, her shoulders sagging.

MORGAN and HUW are still at the table. Huw is pretending to eat. Morgan lays down his knife and fork and stares stonily straight in front of him. Huw scrapes his plate with his fork. After a moment, Morgan smiles a little, without looking at Huw.

MORGAN. Yes, my son. I know you are there.

He looks at Huw kindly and fumbles for his pipe. He begins to fill it as the scene fades out.

PART TWO

The UPSTAIRS BACK BEDROOM of the Morgan House fades in. Beth is making Huw's bed in the foreground. Beyond are the bare springs of the four beds of her other sons. She looks at them sadly as she gives Huw's pillow a final pat. We hear a door slam and running feet on the stairs. Beth turns as Angharad comes bursting into the room. Her face is white, her eyes wide with excitement.

BETH. Goodness gracious, girl!

ANGHARAD (*breathlessly*). Mother—the men are coming up the hill!

BETH. What?

She hurries toward the stairs, followed by Angharad. Beth and Angharad emerge and go to the gate of the house, while all the way down the hill on the street toward the colliery, the women are appearing at their gates, looking anxiously off toward the colliery. In the background the men appear, walking slowly and quietly up the hill. There is no singing.

BETH at the gate is looking toward the men with her hand to her mouth. Then her eyes move to the towering slag heap. The conveyor belt in the distance is moving up the slag heap, dumping the slag on the growing pile. As Beth watches, it slows and comes to a creaking stop.

Beth and Angharad are in the foreground, while the other women are waiting at their gates. Some boys are running excitedly ahead of the men. We begin to hear their cries, unintelligible at first, but then coming more clearly.

SHOUTS. Struck work—the men have struck work! It's a strike!

We get flashes of several of the women reacting: careworn faces contract, a tear or two; a stringy woman gathers her two little children protectively under her arms.

The vanguard of the men comes up the hill. Their faces are grim, but determined. Morgan and Ivor are seen approaching Bronwen's cottage. Bronwen is waiting for Ivor. Ivor and Morgan exchange a look, then Ivor goes to join Bronwen, entering the gate without a word. Morgan moves on toward his own house.

GRUFFYDD'S LODGINGS, a small, dingy house in a street down the hill below the Chapel. Gruffydd and Huw come out from the house, climb the few steps to the street level, and stand staring at the men passing up the street. Gruffydd is coatless and carries a book in his hand with his thumb marking

61

the place, as if he had been interrupted during a lesson. Huw is excited and curious, Gruffydd troubled and sad. The men pass Huw and Gruffydd. The Morgan brothers are prominent in the scene. Inasmuch as they are the strike leaders, they are surrounded by a group of eager, gesticulating men.

HUW (*in a whisper*). What does it mean, Mr. Gruffydd?

GRUFFYDD (*soberly*). It means that something has gone out of this Valley that may never be replaced.

Huw is deeply impressed. He looks off again toward the men. Gruffydd puts his hand kindly on Huw's shoulder.

GRUFFYDD. Home to your father and mother, now. They will need you today.

Huw looks up at Gruffydd for a moment, then nods and runs toward his own house.

At the gate of the MORGAN HOUSE Beth, Morgan and Angharad stand watching silently. Huw comes running, crossing in front of his brothers who are approaching up the hill. The brothers pass by the house without stopping or looking over while the depleted Morgan family watches them pass.

The scene dissolves to the EXTERIOR OF THE MINE WORKS. It is day, but there is no smoke coming from the chimneys, and a big crowd of men is gathered silently outside.

In a VILLAGE STREET the men are standing idly about in knots, some leaning up against the walls. Down the street women are sitting dejectedly on their doorsteps. Children play aimlessly about in the streets, with shrill noise and laughter, unconscious of the tragedy that has befallen the village. The sound of the children's laughter begins to fade as HUW'S VOICE comes in.

HUW'S VOICE. *There is strange it was to go out into the street and find the men there in the daytime. It had a feeling of fright in it.*

HUW comes out of his house and looks off down the street. Against a SECTION OF WALL some men are leaning, arguing quietly. They leave, strolling off down the street, leaving a black mark, shoulder high, on the wall.

Again at the SECTION OF WALL, determined looking women are scrubbing off the black marks with buckets of soapy water.

HUW'S VOICE. *All down the hill, along the walls, a long black mark could be seen where men's shoulders had leaned to rub grease. The women would scrub, but soon it was back, for the men had nowhere else to go.*

The scene dissolves to the EXTERIOR OF THE COLLIERY. It is day, and again the men are standing silently before the colliery. They are now wearing overcoats and scarfs. The wind is howling. Music begins to build in the background.

HUW'S VOICE. *Twenty-two weeks the men were out, as the strike moved into winter. Always the mood of the men grew uglier—as empty bellies and desperation began to conquer reason. Any man who was not their friend became their enemy.*

The scene changes to the EXTERIOR OF THE MORGAN HOUSE. A crowd of depressed, ugly shivering men stands outside. A stone is thrown and it crashes through Morgan's window. Simultaneously, the music reaches a climax and stops.

In the MORGAN PARLOR, Morgan is smoking quietly. He does not move as the stone crashes in, spraying glass at his feet. Beth and Huw, in the background, gasp in dismay.

The scene dissolves to the HILLSIDE. It is night, and Huw and Beth, warmly dressed, are moving up the hill. There is a grim, implacable light in Beth's eyes.

BETH (*gasping*). This way?

Huw nods and points. As they come closer to us, a few drops of rain fall on them. Huw turns up his collar against the rain and stumbles on after his mother, who appears not to notice the rain as she moves purposefully up the hill.

The scene dissolves to ANOTHER LOCATION ON THE HILLSIDE, where Beth and Huw are moving steadily on. A flicker of distant firelight begins to play on their faces. The rain is now coming down harder, and the wind is beginning to blow.

Further along the HILLSIDE, while the rain

is still pouring, a union meeting is in progress. The men are crowded round a circle of Druid stones. They have lit several fires and are all warmly dressed against the cold. Now the meeting is breaking up in the increasing rain. The men are headed toward the path that leads back to the village. At the edge of the crowd, some of the men stop as Beth and Huw appear. She moves determinedly past them in the now driving rain, up to some rocks which form an impromptu speaker's stand. Davy, Ianto, Owen and Gwilym are standing there with other men. They look over in surprise as their mother appears and turns to face the moving men.

BETH (*in a loud, strong voice*). Wait! Wait till you have heard me.

The men, surprised, turn to face her.

BETH looks over the crowd. Her eyes are like Joan of Arc's. Davy and Ianto step toward her, but she ignores them. When she speaks, her voice is low and resolute, like a man's.

BETH. I am Beth Morgan. I have come up here to tell you what I think of you all, because you are talking against my husband.

We see the faces of the men. Some look ashamed, some angry and defiant.

BETH. You are a lot of cowards to go against him. He has done nothing against you and he never would and you know it well. For you to think he is with the owners is not only nonsense but downright wickedness. How some of you can sit in the same Chapel with him I cannot tell. (*Fierce-eyed, she looks over the crowd.*) There is one thing more I will say and that is this. If harm comes to my Gwilym I will find out the men and I will kill them with my hands. And that I will swear by God Almighty.

THE MORGAN BROTHERS staring at her, BETH takes Huw by the arm and leads him away. The men part for her as before, looking after her in the pelting rain. The brothers are seen still staring.

The scene dissolves to BETH and HUW making their way down the HILLSIDE in the dark and rain. The wind is beginning to howl fiercely.

Beth and Huw appear on a STEEP BANK ABOVE THE BROOK. They slip on the bank and fall to the rocks on the edge of the brook where some half-melted snow is banked.

BETH and HUW are in the snow. He lies quiet as she struggles to her knees. The rain has plastered her hair across her face. She is white-faced and panting.

BETH. Huw—

He stirs, pulls himself upright. smiles at her, but dazedly.

HUW. Yes—

BETH. Are you hurt?

HUW. No. I'm all right. (*Bravely*) Up a dando now, Mama.

She laughs in her relief.

BETH. Up a dando, is it? And who was up a dando just now and frightening his mother sick?

She looks around, brushing off the snow.

BETH. Where's the bridge?

HUW (*pointing*). Over by there . . .

They start wearily in the direction Huw has pointed.

HUW'S VOICE. *I was wrong then, for in the blackness I thought we were below the bridge and in truth we were above it.*

Again Beth and Huw stumble forward, pausing to get their bearings. Huw points first in one direction, then another. They start off again in the teeth of the gale.

The scene dissolves to a MOUNTAINSIDE. It is still night. Huw and Beth, almost totally exhausted, are stumbling down a steep place. It is raining fiercely and the wind shrieks through the trees above them. Beth is failing visibly. Huw puts his arm around her, struggling to support her.

HUW'S VOICE. *Hours it seemed, and no feeling or sense was in me—but I was crying to God to help me save my mother and I was helped sure or I could not tell where I found the strength—*

The scene dissolves to a BRIDGE, as Beth and Huw stagger toward it. They reach the bridge. Beth clutches at the rail for support. The wood is rotten and breaks under her weight. She pitches forward into the icy water a few feet below the bridge. Huw gives a frightened gasp and throws himself in after her.

IN THE WATER Beth, inert, is slung around by the swift current. Huw struggles closer to her, as the current brings her up against a rocky point. Gasping with the cold Huw brings her head and shoulders clear of the water. He cannot leave the water himself, but must push against her with all his might to hold her clear of the racing stream.

HUW'S VOICE. *So strong was the cold that for minutes I couldn't breathe—*

HUW, his face contorted, is struggling to hold his mother up as he stands shoulder deep in the icy black water. A faint light appears upon Huw and the inert figure of Beth.

HUW'S VOICE. *How long it was I cannot tell, but there was a weariness of time before I saw a light—*

Huw is desperately holding on as the light grows stronger and dark figures appear in the rain. It is a group of men from the meeting, headed by Davy and Ianto. They have a lantern.

Huw turns, his eyes glistening in the light, and opens his mouth to shout.

HUW'S VOICE. *I tried to shout but my voice was gone from my throat.*

Davy, Ianto and the men, not seeing Huw and his mother, start to cross the bridge. Huw's mouth is open. He is trying to shout against the wind, but he cannot make himself heard. He begins to fail, to slip. Beth's head rolls and she almost goes under the water.

Ianto and Davy with the other men are on the bridge. They are about to leave the bridge and pass on when Ianto almost casually notices that the rail is broken. He stops for a second look, holding the lantern high. Huw is straining mightily to hold Beth above the water. Ianto starts to move away, then raises the lantern once more. As he looks down the stream, his eyes widen in horror. He turns and shouts into the storm.

IANTO (*shouting*). Davy—

He puts down his lantern and plunges forward into the water where Huw is giving his last ounce of strength to hold up his mother until Ianto reaches them. As Ianto pulls them to the bank, Davy and the other men are there to help them to safety. The scene fades out.

The MORGAN PARLOR fades in. It is day, and Bronwen is sitting with some sewing, singing softly. The shades behind her are drawn, so that the light in the room is dim. She raises her head and looks toward the wall bed. We see Huw, unconscious and swathed in bandages, lying in the wall bed. As she looks, his eyes open. He turns his head slowly to look at Bronwen. She puts down her sewing and crosses swiftly over to him.

BRONWEN. Oh—Huw— (*there are tears in her voice.*) There is proud I am to have your name. (*She kisses him softly, straightens and smiles down at him.*)

HUW (*with difficulty*). Mother?

BRONWEN (*cheerfully*). Upstairs—and doing well. The doctor is with her now.

He closes his eyes with a little smile. She stands looking down at him with pity and affection. Morgan, Angharad and Dr. Richards come down the stairs and move over to look down at Huw.

BRONWEN (*whispering*). He was awake just now.

DR. RICHARDS (*in a low voice*). He'll do then. But it's beyond me to say why. You are breeding horses in this family, Mr. Morgan. This boy should be in his coffin, for my part.

MORGAN (*smiling*). Then he's a Morgan, is it?

His hands stray gently to Huw's bandaged shoulder. He touches it proudly and lovingly. In the meantime the Doctor is getting into his overcoat, which Angharad holds for him.

DR. RICHARDS. He should be fed now, Mrs. Ivor—a little soup and some warm smile.

Bronwen nods and goes into the kitchen.

64

Morgan, Angharad and the Doctor go out through the front door.

The Doctor, Angharad and Morgan come out of the MORGAN HOUSE. Morgan closes the door, but not completely. It is left open a crack. Gruffydd comes up the steps, carrying a book.

MORGAN (*to Gruffydd*). Huw was awake just now, and spoke to Bron.

GRUFFYDD (*to Richards*). How long, then, for the little one?

DR. RICHARDS (*pursing his lips*). It's hard to say. His legs were frozen to the bone. A year—two years—quiet like that. But I can't promise he will *ever* walk again—

As HUW's eyes open once more, it is evident that he can hear what is being said outside the door. Dr. Richards' voice comes over:

Nature must take her course—Mr. Gruffydd—

Huw stirs as he hears this. His lips quiver a little; then he looks up. BRONWEN is now in the room with his soup. She looks at Huw anxiously, then hurries to the door.

Bronwen comes out at the FRONT DOOR, closing the door behind her. She addresses herself to the Doctor, with compressed fury.

BRONWEN (*fiercely*). Mind your tongue! I think he heard you.

Disturbed, Morgan, Gruffydd, Angharad and the Doctor look toward the door; then Morgan, Gruffydd, Angharad and Bronwen reenter the house, leaving the Doctor to move down the path.

In the MORGAN PARLOR, Huw is lying in the foreground with eyes bright with tears. Gruffydd comes over, followed by the others, and sits down beside him.

GRUFFYDD (*smiling*). Hello, Huw.

Huw's lips form a soundless "Hello," but his face shows his unhappiness and fear. His eyes turn away from Gruffydd.

GRUFFYDD (*sternly*). Where is the light I thought to see in your eyes? Are you afraid, boy?

Huw turns his mute, appealing eyes back to Gruffydd. Bronwen is shocked by Gruffydd's sternness. She puts her hand on his arm in protest, but Gruffydd shakes it impatiently off.

GRUFFYDD (*relentlessly*). You heard what the doctor said?

A spasm crosses Huw's face and he nods.

GRUFFYDD. And you believed it?

Huw nods again.

GRUFFYDD (*fiercely*). You want to walk again, don't you? (*Huw nods.*) Then you must have faith. And if you have, you *will* walk, no matter what all the doctors say.

Huw looks at him piteously.

HUW (*feebly*). He said Nature must take her course.

GRUFFYDD (*swiftly*). Nature is the handmaiden of the Lord. (*Smiling*) I remember on one or two occasions she was given orders to *change* her course. You know your Scripture, boy?

Huw nods, wide-eyed. Angharad is watching breathlessly, her eyes wide with admiration for Gruffydd.

GRUFFYDD. Then you know that what's been done before can be done again—for you. (*Bending over Huw*) Do you believe me, Huw?

Huw nods again, with shining eyes.

GRUFFYDD (*cheerfully*). Good. You shall see the first daffodil out on the mountain. Will you?

HUW (*weakly, but with a smile*). Indeed I will, sir.

GRUFFYDD. Then you will.

He grins down at Huw, who grins back. Morgan, with tears in his eyes, squeezes Gruffydd's shoulder with emotion and gratitude. Angharad is smiling with starry eyes. Gruffydd shows Huw the book he has brought him.

HUW (*feebly*). "Treasure Island"—

Gruffydd smiles a little as he touches the book.

GRUFFYDD. I could almost wish that I were lying there in your place—if it meant reading this book again for the first time.

Huw looks at the book close to his head with wondering eyes. Gruffydd rises from beside him and goes out of the room. Angharad hesitates a moment, then follows him.

As Gruffydd comes out of the MORGAN HOUSE, Angharad follows.

ANGHARAD (*calling after him*). Mr. Gruffydd—

Gruffydd turns.

ANGHARAD. I couldn't let you go without thanking you.

GRUFFYDD. It was only my duty, girl.

ANGHARAD (*looking at him*). No. It was more than duty.

GRUFFYDD (*his eyes sober*). Yes. He is a fine boy—

He hesitates a moment, looking at her, as if he would like to compliment her personally, but he compromises:

GRUFFYDD. —and you are a fine family.

The look in his eyes is not lost on Angharad. She is still staring up at him with shining eyes. Gruffydd tries to cover his embarrassment.

GRUFFYDD (*gently*). You'd better be going back. You'll catch your death.

ANGHARAD. Yes. (*But she doesn't move.*) Will you be coming to supper soon?

GRUFFYDD. Later—when you are finished with doctors and such.

ANGHARAD (*with a smile*). I will hurry them away then.

GRUFFYDD (*smiling at her*). Good.

He touches his hat and goes, stopping at the gate to look back at her. She looks after him as if unconscious of her surroundings; then she gives a sudden little shudder of cold, drawing her shoulders together. She turns and goes back into the house.

Angharad comes into the MORGAN PARLOR, closing the door. She stands quietly at the door, thinking of Gruffydd. Bronwen, sitting beside Huw, has picked up the book.

She looks up at Angharad with sympathy and comprehension, then turns back to Huw and begins to read.

BRONWEN (*reading*). "Squire Trelawney, Dr. Livesey and the rest of these gentlemen, having asked me to write down the whole particulars about Treasure Island from the beginning to the end, keeping nothing back but the bearings of the island, and that only because there is still treasure not yet lifted, I take up my pen—"

Huw's eyes begin to light up. Bronwen reads on. The scene slowly dissolves to an illustration in "Treasure Island": Jim Hawkins in the crosstrees with Israel Hands, dirk in teeth, climbing the shrouds toward him. Huw's hand leafs the page over.

The scene dissolves back into the MORGAN PARLOR. It is day. HUW, now without bandages, and propped up in bed, is reading, studying, while the normal activity of the house goes on around him.

HUW is seen reading avidly in the MORGAN PARLOR, and superimposed on this picture is a view of the shelf beside the bed. His hands appear, putting the books, one by one, on the shelf:

> TREASURE ISLAND
> IVANHOE
> PICKWICK PAPERS
> BOSWELL'S LIFE OF JOHNSON

As the shelf dissolves, Huw sets down his book and listens, looking up. As a sharp tapping is heard, Huw smiles and taps three times on the wall.

HUW'S VOICE. *For months I lay in the wall bed. I learned. I read. All the noble books which have lived in my mind ever since—and always I hoped and kept my faith.*

For the first months my mother was still upstairs and we could talk to each other with tappings—

In quick succession we see Morgan painting the doorjambs, Angharad hanging fresh curtains, while Huw, in his wall bed, is watching.

The scene dissolves into the MORGAN PARLOR, at night, as Ianto, Davy, Owen and Gwilym are standing before their father in the parlor. Huw is in the wall bed in the background, watching. All involved are very serious. The boys look thin and rather ragged.

HUW'S VOICE. *Then my father began to make preparations—for the doctor told him that soon she would be leaving her bed. New tile for the kitchen—whitewash on our doorstep—new curtains and fresh paint—and, for the occasion—another surprise for my mother.*

MORGAN (*quietly*). My sons, I would like to have you back here to live—

The boys stare as Morgan goes on.

MORGAN. —but on one condition. We shall all be lodgers here.

The boys are silent a moment before answering.

IANTO (*quietly*). How can you be a lodger in your own house?

MORGAN. Because I have no authority. No man shall say he is head of a house unless his word is obeyed. You are grown and entitled to your own opinions. So, we will all be lodgers and your mother will care for all of us.

The boys are silent, looking at the floor.

MORGAN. Will you come?

The boys exchange a look and nod.

MORGAN. Good. It will make your mother very happy. Tomorrow, then.

The boys turn and go out.

Again in the MORGAN PARLOR, in the day, Huw, in his wall bed, is looking toward the stairs with shining eyes. We see THE STAIRCASE, which in Welsh houses is covered, and hear Beth's footsteps dimly on the stairs. Then Beth appears at the bottom of the stairs, assisted by Morgan. She is weak and shaky, and whiter than before, but her eyes are shining. She stands at the foot of the stairs, leaning on Morgan's arm, looking at Huw. Then she slowly crosses over to him, leaving Morgan in the background.

HUW'S VOICE. *Then the great day when at last she came down again into her own house. First her footsteps. Strike and hardship and illness all were forgotten. Four months. Only a ceiling between us,*

yet for four months we hadn't laid eyes on each other. Then she was there, watching me with diamonds in her eyes and her hand to her mouth. Whether to laugh or cry, now . . .

Beth's eyes are full of tears, and she is too moved to speak. She sits beside Huw on the bed, devouring him with her eyes. As he looks at her almost white hair, his hand goes up to it and touches it wonderingly.

BETH. The old snow got into it—

She chokes on the words, kisses him fiercely, and then moves back a little from him as if the better to see him. Morgan tiptoes over to the door, opens it a crack and signals with his hand.

Into the PARLOR, as Beth and Huw look up, comes the sound of Ivor's choir singing. Morgan, smiling proudly, comes back to them. Beth looks toward the door with wonder. Morgan gently helps her to her feet and leads her out, Huw looking after them proudly.

In front of the MORGAN HOUSE the singers, led by Ivor, are massed in the foreground, while Beth and Morgan are on the porch in the background. The Morgan boys are seen watching their mother as they sing in the front row. They have bundles of their belongings with them.

BETH is tremendously affected by the singing, and above all, by the sight of her sons and their bundles. The tears stream down her cheeks, then she buries her face in her husband's shoulder.

BETH (*brokenly*). Oh, Gwil—there is a wife you've got—resting in her bed and letting strangers care for her family.

Morgan smiles and twines a strand of her silver hair round his forefinger.

MORGAN. There is a wife I have got, then.

BETH (*rallying*). Go on with you, boy.

The men finish their song and burst into a shout for Beth. Cries of "Speech!" Morgan pushes her gently forward.

MORGAN. Go on—say something.

BETH (*frightened*). What will I say?

MORGAN. You found something to say

last time you spoke. It should be easier now, with friends.

Beth tries to find words, chokes a little, smiles, holds out her hands to the crowd, hesitates, then blurts:

BETH. Come and eat—everyone—

The people cheer again and begin to troop into the house, paying their respects to Beth as they pass. But her eyes are on her sons and the bundles in their hands. Ianto and Davy, followed by Owen and Gwilym, come up and embrace her silently. She looks at Ianto's bundle with bright eyes, smiling through her tears, then assumes a mask of sternness.

> BETH. There is disgraceful the condition your clothes are in from the lodgings— (*lifting Davy's trouser leg*)—one more step and we would be seeing the back of your leg.
>
> GWILYM. You should see Owen's. One more step and we'd be seeing the back of his neck, indeed.
>
> OWEN (*pushing him*). Shut up, man.

All go into the house.

In the MORGAN PARLOR, the family and guests are trooping in. Some are already making for the food-laden table. Ianto intercepts Morgan in the foreground, and shows his father a newspaper.

> IANTO. Have you seen this?

Morgan takes the paper from Ianto and puts on his glasses to read it. Then, with a twinkle in his eye, he looks over at Huw.

> MORGAN. Well— (*Turning to the guests*) Listen, everyone—listen to this!

The guests gather round. Morgan clears his throat importantly.

> MORGAN. It seems someone has been getting his name in the paper.

He reads proudly from the paper.

> "Handwriting competition. Boys under twelve years of age. First prize of Two Guineas is awarded to Huw Morgan, for an entry of great merit."

A cheer goes up. All eyes turn to Huw in the wall bed. Huw is embarrassed, tries to duck beneath his pillow, but Ianto and Bronwen pull him into the open.

> MORGAN. And that boy has been lying there going on four months and no sound from him but laughing and no words but cheerful. (*Taking off his glasses and wiping them*) I will stay over here to tell you what a good son you are, Huw. If I went to you now, I would be acting very silly, I am afraid.

Bronwen kisses Huw gently.

> BRONWEN. There is a clever old man you are—

HUW reacts to Bronwen's kiss, embarrassed but happy. His eyes are bright, and he touches his cheek where she kissed him.

This scene dissolves to two men with fiddles and Miss Jenkins, a prim spinster who plays the harp. We see the celebration in full swing. These people are hungry and in want, but they are making the most of the occasion and the Morgan's hospitality. A wide-eyed miner receives a cup of tea and some cake from Angharad.

> MINER. Real tea you have.
>
> ANGHARAD. A little weak.
>
> MINER. Weak? Hot water at our house.

Standing near each other are Ianto and Mr. Parry, a bespectacled, ascetic elder who has just finished piling his plate. He takes a mouthful and addresses himself to Ianto.

> PARRY. Ianto—I haven't seen you in Chapel lately.
>
> IANTO. I have been too busy.
>
> PARRY. What business, may I ask?
>
> IANTO (*looking at him*). Mine.

At this a hush falls on the people round them.

> PARRY (*injured*). Only asking a civil question, I was.
>
> IANTO. And having a civil answer. (*Looking at Parry.*) I have been busy with the union.
>
> PARRY (*shaking his head darkly*). Unions are the work of the devil. You will come to no good end.

IANTO (*like ice*). At least I am not *sitting* on it, talking a lot of rubbish in Chapel.

PARRY. Look here—

IANTO (*with an impatient gesture*). Leave it now, or I will say something to be sorry.

He turns away from Parry and finds himself face to face with Gruffydd, who is regarding him steadily. Morgan, Beth and the other Morgan brothers also move into scene, listening intently.

GRUFFYDD. No. This matter requires airing. Ianto—why do you think we of the Chapel talk rubbish?

IANTO. My remark was not aimed at you.

GRUFFYDD (*smiling, but serious*). Then aim it.

IANTO (*deliberately*). Very well. Because you make yourselves out to be shepherds of the flock and yet allow your sheep to live in filth and poverty, and if they try to raise their voices against it, you calm them by saying their suffering is the Will of God. (*With burning scorn*) Sheep indeed! Are we sheep to be herded and sheared by a handful of owners? I was taught that man was made in the image of God! Not a sheep!

MORGAN. Ianto—Mr. Gruffydd healed Huw.

GRUFFYDD (*still looking at Ianto*). Mr. Morgan—Huw healed himself. (*Then to Ianto.*) I have not expressed my views here because I have had no wish to interfere in a family disagreement.

He looks at Morgan challengingly.

MORGAN (*quietly*). You have my permission to speak.

GRUFFYDD. Well, then, here is what I think. First, have your union. You need it.

We see MORGAN listening intently as Gruffydd's voice is heard.

GRUFFYDD'S VOICE. Alone you are weak. Together you are strong.

We get a glimpse of the faces of Ianto, Davy, Owen and Gwilym, listening.

GRUFFYDD'S VOICE. But remember that with strength goes responsibility—to others and to yourselves. (*He is now visible.*) For you cannot conquer injustice with more injustice—only with justice and with the help of God.

ANGHARAD is seen, listening at the tea urn, lips parted and eyes bright. Silence falls on the little group as Gruffydd finishes. He has obviously made a deep impression both on Morgan and on his sons. Then Parry's lips tighten.

PARRY Are you coming outside your position in life, Mr. Gruffydd? Your business is spiritual.

GRUFFYDD (*quietly*). My business is anything that comes between man and the spirit of God.

PARRY (*glowering*). The deacons shall hear that you have been preaching socialism—

Ianto, always ready for a fight, steps up to Parry.

IANTO. Mr. Parry—

Gwilym moves forward.

GWILYM (*hotly*). Loose the old devil's teeth for him!

Morgan quickly steps between them, pushing Ianto and Gwilym back.

MORGAN (*to Ianto*). He is our guest.

He takes Parry's arm and signals to Beth.

MORGAN (*with a grin*). Beth, give Mr. Parry a pint of home brewed, and put his pipe back in his mouth.

BETH (*militantly*). I will give him a good clout with the frying pan.

Parry, abashed, shuts up. Gruffydd smiles and leaves the little group. Morgan and his sons are looking at each other steadily.

IANTO (*to his father*). Can you and your lodgers agree on what we have just heard.

MORGAN (*simply*). I have no lodgers—only sons.

He puts one arm round Ianto's shoulders, the other round Davy's, and signals to Miss Jenkins.

MORGAN. Now, then, Miss Jenkins—a tune. "Comrades in Arms," is it?

The music starts up gaily. All begin to sing, except Parry, who walks off, shaking his head. Angharad, smiling happily, goes into the kitchen with a stack of used plates and sets them on the sink. Gruffydd moves into the foreground, looking at her through the door. Seeing Angharad inspect her fire, then lift the heavy coal scuttle to refill the range, Gruffydd goes into the kitchen.

In the KITCHEN, Angharad is struggling with the heavy scuttle. The singing is heard as Gruffydd comes up to her. She looks at him with a smile.

ANGHARAD. Oh, Mr. Gruffydd—will we always be in your debt? Now you have made us a family again.

GRUFFYDD (*smilingly*). Here—let me—

He takes the scuttle from her and pours some coal into the stove. She is still looking at him. Gruffydd sets down the scuttle and straightens to face Angharad. She sees that his hands are covered with coal.

ANGHARAD. Oh—your hands—there's a pity—

GRUFFYDD (*grinning*). No matter.

He turns his hands to show her the palms. GRUFFYDD'S PALMS, seen in full view, reveal the telltale black lines of one who has worked as a miner. Angharad takes his hands gently, looking at the palms, then up into his eyes.

ANGHARAD. Have you been down the collieries?

GRUFFYDD. Ten years—while I was studying.

ANGHARAD (*moved*). Ten years—

Then she breaks the mood, becoming very businesslike. She moves over toward the sink.

ANGHARAD. A bit of soap, now.

GRUFFYDD. Please don't bother.

He takes a handkerchief from his pocket and begins to scrub at his hands. Angharad turns back to him.

ANGHARAD. There is a man for you— spoiling your good handkerchief.

Gruffydd grins at her. Angharad gets some soap and a piece of rag.

ANGHARAD. Wait, you. You are king in the Chapel, but I will be queen in my own kitchen.

She returns to him and begins to scrub the coal off his hands. Gruffydd's expression has changed. There is no flippancy in his look now. He waits until she has finished, then suddenly speaks, almost as if against his will.

GRUFFYDD. You will be queen wherever you walk.

Angharad looks swiftly up at him, her heart in her eyes. There is a tense pause.

ANGHARAD (*whispering*). What does that mean?

GRUFFYDD (*looking at her*). I should not have said it.

ANGHARAD. Why not?

GRUFFYDD. I have no right to speak to you so.

Angharad continues to look at him, then smiles a little.

ANGHARAD (*softly*). If the right is mine to give—you have it.

They stand looking at each other, deeply moved. Then Bronwen comes into the kitchen with some more plates. She stops short when she sees them, sensing that she has interrupted something, then proceeds to the sink. Gruffydd smiles at Angharad and goes out, Angharad looking after him. Bronwen stands watching her with sympathy and understanding, whereupon Angharad turns to her a little irritably.

ANGHARAD. Well—what are you staring at?

BRONWEN (*smiling*). Let me have my look, girl. (*Then putting her hand on Angharad's arm*) If I were single again —I think I should try to marry Mr. Gruffydd, shame to me or not.

The scene fades out.

70

PART THREE

An early morning scene fades in. The moon is still shining, lights are lit in all the houses, and the men, singing, appear to march up to work. "Men of Harlech" is their song.

In flashes, we see: Beth preparing lunch boxes. Huw waving goodbye to his father and brothers from his wall bed. The rusty colliery gates opening. The men lined up at the gates, being checked through. Singing men entering the colliery. The winding-house wheel, creaking from disuse, as it begins to turn. A puff of steam from a long disused chimney. The conveyor-belt starting. Men waving their lamps to the beat of the music as they march.

> HUW'S VOICE. *Then the strike was settled—with the help of Mr. Gruffydd and my father—with a minimum wage and at least a promise of no more cuts. No victory, but it was good to see my mother's face as she made ready the lunch boxes again. The men went back on the early morning shift. Cold it was, and still dark, but in all the village I think I was the only one to stay in bed. Wheels that had grown rusty turned again, spinning wages for the box on our mantel, which had grown so light—work to wipe out the memory of idleness and hardship. The men were happy going up the hill that morning. —But not all of them—for there were too many now for the jobs open, and some learned that never again would there be work for them in their own Valley—*

AT THE COLLIERY GATE, the mine manager, with a piece of paper in his hand, is approaching the guards at the gate. As the miners file in, he checks something against his tally. The guard begins to close the gate in the faces of the men who are still waiting to go in. The gates close, leaving outside the men who have been shut out. Prominent among them are Owen and Gwilym, who are standing grim-faced with the other men, silent, hard-eyed.

The scene dissolves to the MORGAN PARLOR. Morgan, Ivor, Ianto, Davy, Owen and Gwilym are assembled—a council of war. Huw, in his wall bed, is in the background.

OWEN. It is the same all over South Wales. In Cardiff, the men are standing in line to have bread from the government. (*Shaking his head*) Not for us. We will have our share of the box and go.

MORGAN. Where?

OWEN (*quietly*). America.

Morgan's shoulders sag. He turns slowly to the mantelpiece, takes the box, and sets it down on the table. He opens the cover and stands looking down into it. The others gather round. Morgan slowly takes out two small stacks of sovereigns, setting one before Owen and one before Gwilym. Then Ianto speaks:

IANTO (*quietly*). My share, too, Owen.

DAVY (*quickly*). And mine.

OWEN. No. Our own. We will take no charity.

IANTO (*roughly*). Not charity, man. Sense.

GWILYM (*stubbornly*). No. Only our own.

Owen also shakes his head with finality. Morgan closes the box with a snap, then turns to Owen and Gwilym.

MORGAN. Say nothing to your mother. Let this day be over, first.

Suddenly they hear Beth's voice.

BETH'S VOICE. Never mind saying nothing.

They all turn. The little group stands round the table, taking in Beth as she moves slowly toward them from the kitchen door, where she has been standing.

BETH. I heard.

Beth reaches Owen and Gwilym. The tears spring to her eyes as she embraces them.

BETH (*brokenly*). America—America—my babies—

After a moment Morgan gently withdraws Beth from her two sons, holding her in his arms for a moment. He looks at the boys.

MORGAN. Shall we read a chapter, my sons?

OWEN. What shall we have?

MORGAN. Isaiah, fifty-five. "Ho every one that thirsteth, come ye to the waters, and he that hath no money, come ye, buy and eat."

Owen crosses to get the Bible from the shelf on the mantel. Beth, unable to stand any more, moves over toward Huw and sits down on the bed beside him. She is crying. Huw tries awkwardly to comfort her.

BETH (tragically). This is only the beginning. Owen and Gwil first—then all of you will go—one after the other—all of you!

HUW (stoutly). I will never leave you, Mama—

Beth takes him by the shoulders, and stares into his eyes.

BETH. Yes, Huw. If you should ever leave me, I will be sorry I ever had babies.

HUW (wondering). Why did you have them?

BETH (with a twist of her lips). Goodness gracious, boy! Why, indeed? To keep my hands in water and my face to the fire, perhaps.

Morgan is seen marking his place in the Bible. His sons are grouped round him. Before Morgan can begin to read, though, they hear a commotion out in the street. They all look up, as they hear loud, excited voices shouting something we cannot distinguish. One of the boys opens the door and all go out in the street.

Morgan and his sons are standing outside the house, as Beth comes curiously out to join them. Approaching the house is about half the village following the figure of Dai Ellis, the postman, who carries a letter high in his hand. The villagers are shouting and chattering to each other.

IANTO. What is it?

MORGAN. They're coming here.

They exchange a look, almost as if this might be a lynching party come to get them. The villagers approach behind the postman. Dai Ellis, his hand trembling with excitement, holds up the letter. He tries to speak but his vocal chords are paralyzed with excitement. He stutters impotently.

IANTO (impatiently). What's with you, man?

Ellis finally produces words:

DAI ELLIS (his voice breaking into a falsetto squeak). From Windsor Castle it is—

He hands the letter to Ivor. The Morgans, seen as a group, are tremendously excited. Ivor takes the letter. The villagers gather close round as Ivor rips it open with impatient fingers. He begins to read from the letter.

IVOR (in a trembling voice). Mr. Ivor Morgan is commanded to appear before her Majesty at Windsor Castle with chosen members of his choir.

A great shout goes up from the assembled villagers. Morgan, powerfully affected, grabs Ivor's shoulder.

MORGAN. To sing before the Queen. (With quiet pride.) My son, I never thought to see the beautiful day. (Then with animation.) Ianto, Davy—(to the assembled villagers)—all of you. Fetch everyone from all the Valleys round. (To the postman.) Dai Ellis, get your trap and to town to spread the news. Davy—over to the other collieries—invite everybody—it's a celebration, tell them. Ianto—down to the Three Bells for beer. Open house tonight—for all who will come.

Then his eye catches sight of Owen and Gwilym standing together. There is a break in his voice as he addresses them.

MORGAN. My sons. You shall have a send-off worthy of Morgans.

IN THE STREET, the people are running excitedly off in different directions. Dai Ellis jumps into his trap, which stands in front of the post office, and whips his horse off into a gallop.

The scene dissolves to an exterior view of the VILLAGE at night. The windows are all lit and people lean in them, looking out. The party is assembled. The street is filled with celebrating people. Beer is flowing freely. All are singing the last bars of a gay Welsh song. As the song finishes, Morgan climbs up on the wall in front of the CHAPEL with Ivor. (The choir is assembled in the street.) He holds up his hand for silence. When he gets it he begins to pray, simply and sincerely.

> MORGAN. O Heavenly Father, I give thanks from the heart to live this day. I give thanks for all I have, and I do give thanks for this new blessing. For you are Our Father, but we look to our Queen as our mother. Comfort her in her troubles, O God, and let her mighty worries trouble not more than she shall bear in her age. And let sweetness and power and spirit be given to these voices that will sing at her command. And may Ivor have strength to acquit himself with honour. Amen.

A deep, reverent, "Amen" goes up in the street.

Morgan climbs down from the wall and joins Beth. Then Ivor raises his hand and brings it down sharply. The tenors sing the first line of "God Save the Queen." Sopranos join the tenors with the second line.

HUW is seen in his wall bed, eyes shining. Bron and Angharad are with him. The window is open. Baritones, bass and alto come in with tenor and soprano. The whole CHOIR is seen singing. All the voices are now in.

Morgan is singing along with the choir, but Beth is silent. She is looking steadily, with tears in her eyes, out of the scene. We follow the direction of her glance. THE MORGAN BROTHERS are in the front line of the choir, singing with the rest. We see Owen and Gwilym closely as the anthem goes into its final chords.

The whole VILLAGE is seen as the anthem comes to its close.

The scene fades out.

PART FOUR

The INTERIOR OF THE CHAPEL fades in. Gruffydd is leading the congregation in the closing hymn of the service. The hymn stops and the men begin to pick up their hats.

GRUFFYDD (soberly). Will you please remain in your places? There is a meeting of the deacons.

A little buzz of conversation goes up as the people resume their seats. The deacons, mostly elderly men, stalk stiffly up to the front of the Chapel. Morgan is among the deacons. Gruffydd relinquishes his place at the lectern to Mr. Parry and then walks slowly down the aisle, his head bent. He passes Angharad, who is sitting on the aisle, and moves to the back of the Chapel. Mr. Parry, spokesman for the deacons, stands forward.

PARRY (sternly). Meillyn Lewis—step forward.

A girl, whom we have not seen before, stumbles past Angharad. She is sobbing violently into her handkerchief, which covers her face. She steps before the assembled deacons.

PARRY (looking down at her). Your sins have found you out, and now you must pay the price of all women like you. You have brought a child into the world against the commandment.

ANGHARAD is seen staring, white-faced, shocked and pitying. GRUFFYDD, at the back, is expressionless but manifestly uncomfortable. The faces of the deacons look stern. Morgan alone among them looks disturbed and unhappy.

PARRRY (continuing). Prayer is wasted on your sort. You shall be cast forth into the outer darkness till you have learned your lesson. Meillyn Lewis, do you admit your sin?

MEILLYN LEWIS sobs out something like "Yes."

ANGHARAD rises slowly to her feet.

PARRY looks sternly down at Meillyn Lewis.

PARRY. Then prepare to suffer your punishment—

Angharad's voice rings out.

ANGHARAD. Stop it! Stop it! Let her alone —you hypocrites!

It is as if the meeting had been struck by lightning. Meillyn Lewis, mouth open, tears dripping from her eyes, is staring at Angharad. The deacons are also staring, still too amazed to be angry. Then Morgan moves. His face is white with fury. He strides over to Angharad.

MORGAN (furiously). Angharad—you—

Gruffydd steps quickly between them. He puts his hand on Morgan's arm.

GRUFFYDD (looking at Angharad). Leave it now, Mr. Morgan.

He urges Angharad gently away, Morgan staring after them. Gruffydd and Angharad exit from the Chapel, with all the congregation staring.

Angharad and Gruffydd come out of the Chapel. She is still white and shaken. He looks at her soberly. At a little distance from them an old, poorly dressed woman, Meillyn Lewis's mother, is waiting nervously, holding a baby. Angharad with an angry gesture raises her eyes to Gruffydd's.

ANGHARAD (passionately). How could you stand there and watch them? Cruel old men—groaning and nodding to hurt her more. That isn't the Word of God! "Go thou, and sin no more," Jesus said.

GRUFFYDD (sadly). You know your Bible too well—and life too little.

ANGHARAD (stormily). I know enough of life to know that Meillyn Lewis is no worse than I am!

GRUFFYDD. Angharad!

ANGHARAD. What do the deacons know about it? (Clenching her fists) What do you know about what could happen to a poor girl when she loves a man so much that even to lose sight of him for a moment is torture!

Her eyes try to hold him, for she is now referring to her own love for him. But Gruffydd will not meet the issue.

GRUFFYDD. It was cruel, but you must realize that the men of the Valleys here have made their homes, lived and died with no help from any government of men—no authority but the Bible. If it has produced hypocrites and Pharisees the fault is with the human race. Men are not angels.

ANGHARAD. They were like devils today! My father, too. (Accusingly) And you stood by and let them.

Gruffydd frowns. He is as deeply moved as Angharad, but finds his predicament difficult to explain to her.

GRUFFYDD. It's their Chapel. I am only its servant. If I spoke out now—they could put me out to preach in the hedges with only the sparrows to listen.

ANGHARAD. But you will speak out against it?

GRUFFYDD (nodding gravely). When the time is ripe. When the ground is prepared. Believe me.

She softens. Their eyes meet and hold. Then both turn as the door of the Chapel opens in the background and Meillyn Lewis stumbles out. She runs to her mother, crying. Other people begin to appear from the Chapel. Meillyn takes the baby and kisses it. She and her mother cling to each other forlornly and start to walk slowly away. ANGHARAD AND GRUFFYDD are looking after them with compassion. With one accord they start to move after Meillyn and her mother. Angharad calls gently:

ANGHARAD. Meillyn—

The scene fades out.

PART FIVE

The MORGAN PARLOR fades in. Huw is reading in his wall bed. Beth is straightening up the room. Huw looks up as sunlight falls across him from the opening front door and his face lights up as he sees Gruffydd standing, framed in the sunlight. There is something portentous in his manner. His face is very grave. Beth moves into the scene. She is surprised to see Gruffydd.

BETH. Good morning, dear Mr. Gruffydd. There is good to see you. Angharad is down to market.

Gruffydd does not move. His eyes remain searchingly on Huw.

GRUFFYDD (looking at Huw). I have come for Huw.

BETH (surprised). For Huw?

She looks over at Huw, who is smiling. He has sensed why Gruffydd is here. He is smiling—but frightened and a little in awe.

HUW. The daffodils are out, Mama.

BETH (with her heart in her eyes). Oh, Huw—

She crosses over to him, clutching her hands in her apron. Then Gruffydd, still with his eyes on Huw, advances.

GRUFFYDD. Where are your clothes, Huw?

HUW. Under my pillow, sir.

BETH. Your pillow?

HUW. For these months—ready for to-day.

GRUFFYDD (smiling). Come you, then— You shall bring back a posy fit for a queen for your brave mother—

HUW (eyes shining). Indeed, I will—

Beth is too stunned to move. Gruffydd starts to help Huw out from under the covers, and to retrieve his clothes from under the pillow.

The scene dissolves to the HILLSIDE. It is a bright, windy morning. A patch of daffodils is nodding in the wind. In the background Gruffydd is carrying Huw on his shoulders. Silhouetted against the skyline, they come close to the daffodils. Gruffydd gently lowers Huw to his feet and sup-

ports him there, while both look at the flowers. They smile at each other. Gruffydd carefully releases Huw and moves a few steps away from him, then turns and holds out his hands to Huw.

GRUFFYDD. Now, then—over to me—

Slowly, painfully, Huw moves one leg forward, and brings the other up to join it. Then he sways as if about to fall. Gruffydd steps quickly forward to support him, but Huw waves him away with a grin.

HUW (a little breathless). I'm all right—

He takes two more steps, which bring him to Gruffydd. They grin at each other, and Gruffydd takes hold or him.

GRUFFYDD. Enough, now. (Looking at Huw searchingly, and speaking gravely.) You have been lucky, Huw. Lucky to suffer and lucky to spend these weary months in your bed. For so God has given you the chance to make spirit within yourself. And as your father cleans his lamp to have good light, so keep clean your spirit.

HUW. How, Mr. Gruffydd?

GRUFFYDD. By prayer, my son. And I don't mean mumbling, or shouting, or wallowing like a hog in religious sentiments. Prayer is only another name for good, clean, direct thinking. When you pray, think well what you are saying, and make your thoughts into things that are solid. In that manner, your prayer will have strength, and that strength shall become part of you, mind, body and spirit.

Huw looks up at him, deeply impressed. Then Gruffydd smiles.

GRUFFYDD. And the first duty of your new legs shall be to carry you to Chapel next Sunday.

The scene dissolves to the CHAPEL with the Morgan family approaching it in the daylight. Morgan and Beth are not in evidence. In the group are Angharad, Ianto, Davy and Huw, who is now limping painfully, with the aid of Davy.

NEAR THE CHAPEL ENTRANCE, IESTYN EVANS, a rather supercilious young man, and dressed—even overdressed—in the height of fashion, is lounging on the Chapel green. He looks over and sees Angharad. He steps forward and raises his hat.

IESTYN. Hello, Angharad.

Ianto and Davy step in front of their sister.

IANTO (*with dangerous quiet*). Who are you talking to?

IESTYN (*casually*). Angharad. Your sister, perhaps.

Ianto knocks him down with one punch. IESTYN, out cold, crashes against the Chapel entrance and winds up sitting on the ground. His fall dislodges the sign announcing the subject of the sermon. It falls across him, bearing the legend:

"LOVE YE ONE ANOTHER"

Ianto, his brothers and Angharad are all looking down at Iestyn. Angharad then goes for Ianto with clawed fingers.

ANGHARAD. You devil.

Davy catches Angharad and pulls her back from Ianto, who looks at his knuckles, then at the fallen Iestyn.

IANTO (*quietly*). I will not have my sister treated like a pit-woman. His father may own the colliery, but if he wants to speak to you, let him ask permission. We have a home and he knows well where it is.

The Chapel-goers are now crowded round Iestyn, who is being helped to his feet by Morgan and Iestyn's father, Christmas Evans. They approach Ianto and the others.

EVANS. Did you hit my son?

IANTO. I did.

MORGAN. Here at Chapel?

IANTO (*looking at Iestyn*). That's where he was. Buttonhole and all.

EVANS. I will have you in court, young man!

IESTYN (*to Ianto, groggy but defiant*). Doubtless you had a reason.

IANTO. Doubtless. And doubtless I will break your neck if I have another reason.

MORGAN. Why did you hit him?

IANTO. Let *him* tell you.

Morgan looks at Iestyn, who speaks after a moment's hesitation.

IESTYN. I spoke to your daughter, sir.

EVANS (*his eyebrows go up*). You *spoke* to her?

IESTYN (*somewhat chastened*). Yes, sir.

Evans turns to Ianto and holds out his hand.

EVANS. Ianto, I am sorry for what I said. (*Glaring at Iestyn*) If a man spoke to Iestyn's sister, murder would be done.

He pushes Iestyn toward Ianto.

EVANS. Now, then—shake hands—no malice anywhere, is it?

They shake hands, but gingerly, like a couple of prize fighters. Then Iestyn bows to Morgan.

IESTYN. I will call to ask your permission tomorrow evening, Mr. Morgan.

MORGAN. Good, I will wait for you.

The sound of organ music, the processional, comes from the Chapel. All adjust themselves and start into the Chapel. Moving toward the entrance, Ianto and Iestyn enter together, walking side by side, but still stiff toward each other. Christmas Evans follows and after him Davy and Huw. Then Beth and Morgan. As Beth and Morgan come close, we see that there are tears in her eyes. Her husband notices them.

MORGAN (*in a whisper*). What ails you, girl?

BETH (*sniffing*). Too young—even to be *thinking* of marriage—

MORGAN (*cocking a humorous eye at her*). How old were you?

BETH (*wiping her eyes*). Much older, boy.

MORGAN. Go on with you, girl. You were younger still than Angharad.

Angharad follows them. She comes face to face with Gruffydd, hesitates a moment, then goes into the Chapel.

The scene dissolves into the MORGAN KITCHEN, at night. ANGHARAD is looking through the open door toward a group in the parlor. Her expression is bewildered and unhappy as we hear Gruffydd's voice.

GRUFFYDD'S VOICE. The bath holds one hundred gallons. "A" fills the bath at the rate of twenty gallons a minute. "B" at the rate of ten gallons a minute.

We see Gruffydd, Morgan and Bronwen coaching Huw, who sits at a table piled with books and papers. Beth sits nearby, busy with her sewing. Gruffydd is giving Huw a problem. Huw takes notes as Gruffydd talks.

GRUFFYDD. "C" is a hole which empties the bath at five gallons a minute. Got it? (*Huw nods.*) How long to fill the bath?

Beth clicks her tongue disapprovingly so that they all turn to look at her.

BETH. There is silly. Trying to fill a bath with holes in it, indeed.

MORGAN. A sum it is, my girl. A sum. A problem for the mind. For his examination into school next month.

BETH (*doggedly*). That old National School. There is silly their sums are with them. Who would pour water in an old bath with holes? Who would think of it, but a madman?

MORGAN (*his eyes seeking heaven*). It is to see if the boy can calculate, girl. Figures, nothing else. How many gallons and how long.

BETH. In a bath full of holes.

She throws her sewing at her workbasket, misses it and throws it again twice as hard. Morgan regards her with an exasperated grin, then turns to Gruffydd, who is smiling covertly.

MORGAN. Now I know why I have such a tribe of sons. It is you. Beth Morgan

is the cause. Look you, Mr. Gruffydd. Have you got something else?

GRUFFYDD. The decimal point, Mr. Morgan.

MORGAN. The decimal point, then— (*with a look at Beth*)—and peace in my house.

BETH (*calmly*). Go and scratch.

She rises, putting her work away. Gruffydd also gets up.

GRUFFYDD (*with a smile*). It is late, now. I will be going. (*Putting his hand on Huw's shoulder*) We will follow the decimal point tomorrow night. (*Bowing to Morgan and Beth*) Good night.

They bid him goodnight and Morgan puts out the lamp on the table, which leaves only the little lamp near Huw's wall bed. He and Beth go up the stairs as Gruffydd goes to the door, signalling to Huw to follow him. Huw hobbles after Gruffydd.

Gruffydd and Huw come out of the MORGAN HOUSE. From his pocket Gruffydd takes a beautiful pencil box which he presents to Huw.

GRUFFYDD. It was mine and my father's.

HUW (*deeply appreciative*). There is beautiful, Mr. Gruffydd.

We see the PENCIL BOX IN GRUFFYDD'S HANDS. The hands slide the lid back and forth.

GRUFFYDD'S VOICE. See how he joined it— and the pattern of grained woods on the lid and round the sides. Labor and love —therefore beauty.

He gives the box to Huw.

GRUFFYDD. It's yours—for when you go to school.

HUW (*in an awed whisper*). Mr. Gruffydd—

GRUFFYDD. Take care of it, then—

HUW (*overwhelmed*). Oh, I will, sir— thank you—

GRUFFYDD. You're having an opportunity none of your brothers had—to get yourself a good education in a good school. Be worthy of it, Huw.

HUW. I'll try, sir.

GRUFFYDD. Good. You will come tomorrow? I promised your father we would make him a frame for the picture Queen Victoria gave to Ivor.

HUW. Yes, sir.

GRUFFYDD (*smiles*). Good night then— and God bless you.

HUW. Good night, sir.

Gruffydd goes down the path. Huw goes back into the house and closes the door.

In the MORGAN PARLOR, Huw is hobbling back over toward his bed, looking at the pencil box with wide eyes. He sets it down beside the bed and begins to undress.

In BETH AND MORGAN'S BEDROOM, at night, Beth, in her old-fashioned nightgown, is just climbing into the double bed and pulling up the covers. Morgan, in an equally old-fashioned nightshirt, is approaching the bed with a lighted candle, which he sets beside the bed.

BETH (*frowning a little*). Gwil—who is in charge of this decimal point?

MORGAN (*pleading*). Look, Beth, my little one, leave it now, or else it will be morning and us fit for bedlam, both.

BETH. But who thought of it?

MORGAN. I don't know. The French, I think.

BETH. Well, no wonder! Those old Frenchies, is it?

MORGAN (*climbing into bed*). There is an old beauty you are. Go to sleep now before I will push you on the floor.

Beth turns over on her side.

BETH (*muttering, as she turns*). With Frenchies and old baths full of holes, what will come to the boy? What will come to the country, indeed?

MORGAN. Let the Old Queen in Windsor Castle worry over that.

Beth, apparently mollified, settles herself in the bed and closes her eyes. Morgan reaches over to pinch out the candle, but before

he can do so, Beth's eyes open and she speaks once more.

BETH. Gwil—

MORGAN (*impatiently*). Yes, girl?

BETH (*dreamily*). I wonder does the Queen know about this decimal point?

MORGAN. Well, devil throw smoke!

He pinches out the light.

The scene dissolves to GRUFFYDD'S LODGINGS, at night. It is a combination study, bedroom and carpentry shop. (For woodworking is Gruffydd's hobby.) Now, of course, we can see nothing, for the room is dark. Gruffydd enters, crosses to his desk and lights the lamp upon it. Then he stops short. The light reveals Angharad standing there. Her mood is strange, unnaturally calm. For a moment they are silent.

GRUFFYDD (*quietly*). You shouldn't be here.

ANGHARAD. I couldn't spend another night without knowing. (*Looking up at him with tortured eyes*) What has happened? Is something wrong?

GRUFFYDD. Wrong?

ANGHARAD. You know what I mean. Why have you changed towards me? Why am I a stranger now? Have I done anything?

GRUFFYDD. No—the blame is mine. Your mother spoke to me after Chapel. She is happy to think you will be having plenty all your days.

ANGHARAD (*with a note of scorn*). Iestyn Evans.

GRUFFYDD (*looking at her*). You could do no better.

ANGHARAD (*quietly*). I don't want him. I want you.

GRUFFYDD (*quietly*). Angharad—I have spent nights too—trying to think this out. When I took up this work, I knew what it meant. It meant devotion—and sacrifice. It meant making it my whole life—to the exclusion of everything else. That I was perfectly willing to do. But to share it with another— (*With sudden emotion*) Do you think I will have you going threadbare all your life? Depending on the charity of others for your good meals? Our children growing up in cast-off clothing—and ourselves thanking God for parenthood in a house full of bits? (*Shaking his head with determination*) No—I can bear with such a life for the sake of my work. (*Suddenly savage*) But I think I would start to kill if I saw the white come into your hair twenty years before its time.

Angharad comes close, looking up at him with misty eyes. She understands the significance of his last remark.

ANGHARAD (*softly*). Why?

He doesn't answer.

ANGHARAD (*more insistently*). Why would you start to kill?

Gruffydd averts his eyes. She moves even closer to him.

ANGHARAD. Are you a man—or a saint?

GRUFFYDD (*in a low voice*). I am no saint —but I have a duty towards you. Let me do it.

Angharad realizes that she has made no impression on him.

ANGHARAD (*brokenly—tearfully*). Did I come here to hear sermons about your duty?

He does not move. She stares at him for another moment, then turns on her heel and goes out. Gruffydd stands looking after her.

Angharad comes swiftly out of GRUFFYDD's LODGINGS. We watch her as she rounds the corner. Then she bursts into sobs as she hurries along. The scene fades out.

The interior of GRUFFYDD's LODGINGS fades in. It is day. We see Gruffydd's work bench, at which Huw and Gruffydd are busy making the picture frame. Huw shows Gruffydd the piece he has been working on.

GRUFFYDD. Good. Now a piece for the molding—about two feet.

HUW. Yes, sir.

He hunts around on the bench for a piece of wood and then looks up at Gruffydd.

HUW. Will I ever be rich, Mr. Gruffydd?

GRUFFYDD (*gravely*). You *are* rich, Huw.

HUW. Me? Oh, no, Mr. Gruffydd.

GRUFFYDD. What do you want, then?

Huw is silent, trying to think what he wants.

GRUFFYDD (*smiling*). If you cannot think what you want, think how you would feel if you lost what you have. Your father and mother. Your brothers and sisters. Your home. Would you feel poor if you lost them? (*Huw nods.*) Then you are rich in possessing them. And that is the real wealth, Huw—because it was earned by love.

Huw is deeply impressed by what Gruffydd has said, but he is still struggling with his thoughts about Gruffydd and Angharad. He hesitates a moment, then blurts out:

HUW. But you will never have either kind of wealth! You can't marry Angharad because you have no money.

Gruffydd is startled by Huw's outburst. But as Huw looks up at him challengingly, Gruffydd speaks quietly:

GRUFFYDD (*kindly*). Who has been talking to you, Huw?

HUW. Bron—and—I have heard other talk.

Gruffydd's face goes stern for a moment, then he smiles a little wistfully and lays his hand affectionately on Huw's shoulder. After a moment he turns and goes slowly to the window.

GRUFFYDD is at the window, and Huw in the background is watching him. Gruffydd is silent for a moment, then speaks as much to himself as to Huw.

GRUFFYDD (*quietly, but with bitterness*). Perhaps there is still a third kind of wealth. Perhaps a man is wrong to ask more for himself than the opportunity to serve his God—

The scene dissolves to the EXTERIOR OF THE

CHAPEL on a bright spring day. The Chapel door is seen. The whole Valley is out, in much the same spirit as for Bronwen and Ivor's wedding earlier. The villagers are cheering and throwing rice at a bride and groom emerging from the Chapel. In the close foreground stands a smart, open carriage, driven by a coachman, who is not in too resplendent uniform. Until the bride and groom come close, we do not see who they are. They are ducking, shielding their faces from the rice. The coachman jumps down to help them into their carriage and we see that they are Iestyn and Angharad. Iestyn is smiling proudly. Angharad's face is blank. Iestyn helps her into the carriage and climbs in beside her. He takes her hand possessively.

IESTYN. My darling—you shall have everything in the world.

He kisses her while the celebrants round the carriage laugh and cheer. She responds, but automatically, without any real warmth.

Her eyes go past him back to the Chapel, then the coachman cracks his whip and, with a jerk, the carriage moves out of sight. The celebrants crowd into the foreground waving after the carriage. The people gathered at the Chapel begin to leave, moving down into the street. Near the Chapel door are the last of them, Morgan, Beth and Huw. They start to move slowly away from the Chapel. Beth is crying, Morgan has his arm around her. Huw looks at his mother, then back toward the open Chapel door. His face is very grave. They go out of scene as the door comes into view.

From the door, GRUFFYDD is seen moving methodically about at the front of the Chapel, putting away his book, extinguishing a candle, straightening the cloth on the lectern. He finishes his work and walks slowly forward. As he comes close, we see that his face is grave and self-contained. Gruffydd comes out through the door, gently closing it, turns and goes out of our vision, as the scene fades out.

PART SIX

The INTERIOR OF THE SCHOOL CLASSROOM fades in. It is day. Children, boys and girls, are filing into the classroom as if from recess. A group of them come into the foreground. One of them, Mervyn Phillips, is a rather bullying, heavy type. They stop by a desk and look down. On the desk are Huw's books and the pencil-box given him by Mr. Gruffydd. The boys exchange mischievous looks. Mervyn Phillips takes up the pencil-box and cracks it against the desk. Others begin to tear Huw's books and to pour ink on them. One of the boys looks back over his shoulder.

BOY. Look out, here he comes.

They scatter to their own desks. Huw comes up to his desk. As HUW looks down, his eyes widen, then his fists clench and tears start in his eyes. He looks up and faces them.

HUW. I'll fight you all.

Some of the boys laugh, some sneer at him.

MERVYN PHILLIPS. Dirty coal miner!

HUW. You first.

Then Huw begins to sob, though he tries to fight the sobs back. He tries to mop the pencil-box with his clean handkerchief, then puts the handkerchief to his eyes, leaving a black smudge on his face. His fists clenched,

he starts toward Mervyn Phillips. One of the boys calls out warningly.

BOY. Look out!

All take their seats hastily as the sound of the door opening is heard. JONAS, the master has entered the room. He is an unpleasant man, young, but heavy, and pedantic, with a sneering manner and an affected English drawl. He looks at the class and notices Huw's rumpled, tearful condition. He walks slowly over to him and stands looking down at him. Huw looks defiantly up at him, rising slowly.

JONAS. You are the new boy? (*With an unpleasant smile*) What a dirty little sweep it is.

He pulls Huw's handkerchief from his

pocket and inspects it disapprovingly, holding it daintily between two fingers.

HUW (*rebelliously*). It was clean when I left home—

The smile, as if by magic, leaves Jonas' face.

JONAS. You will address me as "sir" or I will put a stick about you. Now sit down. If you expect to stay with us you will have to be more civilized.

Mutiny wells up in Huw. He glares fiercely at Jonas. Jonas turns away and moves up to the head of the class.

The scene dissolves to the SCHOOLYARD. The children are pouring out for midday recess, a jostling crowd. Huw and Mervyn Phillips approach each other.

MERVYN. Fight me, will you?

He swings wildly at Huw. Huw swings back, but is no match for Phillips. He goes down under a rain of blows, comes up with his nose and mouth bleeding and goes down again. This time Mervyn jumps on him and pummels him on the ground. The boys who have gathered round the fight are all for Mervyn. They cheer him on as he pounds Huw.

The scene dissolves to the EXTERIOR OF THE MORGAN HOUSE. It is early evening. Huw, battered and bedraggled, slowly approaches the house. He carries his broken pencil-box and ink-stained books. His clothes are smudged and torn. His face is a battered mass with a black eye and bloody nose and several cuts. He looks at the front door, then turns and goes past the house to sneak in the back way. He stops at the sound of Davy's voice.

DAVY'S VOICE. Here he is.

Ianto and the other brothers are coming out of the shed, where they have been washing. They come up to Huw. Ianto sees Huw's face and whistles. He lifts Huw's chin. Huw tries frantically to think of a plausible lie.

HUW. I—I fell on the mountain.

IANTO (*grimly*). Did you win?

HUW (*honestly*). No.

Ianto looks at Davy.

IANTO. Where will we find Dai Bando?

DAVY. At the Three Bells, likely.

IANTO. Come.

They leave. Huw turns to the HOUSE. Beth is coming out with a pail of slops. She sees Huw and stares. She puts down the pail and runs to him, taking him in her arms, tears in her eyes.

BETH. Oh, Huw—what have they done to you?

Morgan comes out of the house and crosses to Huw. He looks gravely at his son, then takes him by the arm.

MORGAN. Come with me.

He leads him into the house. Beth, fearful that Morgan is going to give Huw a licking, hurries after him.

BETH. Gwilym—Gwilym—

In the MORGAN PARLOR, Morgan and Huw come in, followed by Beth, protesting. Morgan says nothing. He stops before the mantelpiece, takes down the box and sets it on the table. He takes a few coins from it and looks at Huw.

MORGAN. Are you willing to go back to school tomorrow?

HUW. Yes, sir.

MORGAN. Good. From tonight you shall have a penny for every mark on your face, sixpence for a bloody nose, a shilling for a black eye, and two shillings for a broken nose.

He gives some coins to Huw, Beth already listening with growing disapproval.

BETH. Gwilym—stop it. (*To Huw*) Fight again and when you come home not a word shall you have from me. Not a look. (*Fiercely*) Break your old nose, then! Break your mother's heart every time you go from the house!

MORGAN. A boy must fight, Beth.

BETH. Fight, is it? Another beating like that one and he will be dead.

MORGAN (*smiling*). He has had no beating. A hiding—yes—but no beating. He shall come for more until *he* is giving the beating, is it?

The two are glaring at each other, the first serious disagreement we have seen between them. Then the door opens and Dai Bando comes in with Ianto and Davy. Dai is a prize fighter, short, but as broad as he is tall, with long arms, only one or two teeth in his head. He bears the marks of a hundred fights on his face and wears a patch over one eye. The other eye is a mere slit between puffs. Morgan and Beth turn. Morgan is glad to see Dai, but Beth shows her disapproval from the beginning. Dai, however, is too simple to notice this. He is like a big friendly dog as he comes beaming across to them, walking with the curious, mincing prize fighter's walk. Following Dai now, and throughout the picture, is Cyfartha, a mild little man with violently checked clothes and an enormous curved pipe. He is Dai's manager, second, guide, philosopher and friend.

DAI (*heartily*). Good evening, Mrs. Morgan. (*To Morgan*) Good evening, sir.

CYFARTHA (*to everyone*). Good evening to you.

Morgan smiles pleasantly and shakes hands, but Beth only looks at Dai coldly. Ianto pushes Huw gently toward Dai.

IANTO (*to Huw*). Dai is going to teach you to box.

DAI (*correcting him*). To fight, first. Too many call themselves boxers who are not even fighters. (*Impressively*) Boxing is an art, is it?

Cyfartha nods agreement and pantomimes a punch. Beth lets out an emphatic snort of disapproval. Morgan tries to cover her rudeness.

MORGAN. Get on with you, girl. Won't you offer Dai and Cyfartha a cup of tea, now?

CYFARTHA (*hastily*). No—no. No tea, Mrs. Morgan. In training he is—for the match with Big Shoni. Only beer for him. A pint of your good home-brewed, Mrs. Morgan, is it?

He holds up two fingers suggestively. Beth, with obvious bad grace, moves toward the kitchen, glowering. Dai's manner becomes professional.

DAI (*to Huw*). Now, then. Strip off, boy.

Huw unbuttons his shirt.

At the KITCHEN DOOR Morgan intercepts Beth.

MORGAN (*whispering*). What's with you, girl?

BETH (*in a fierce whisper*). Frenchies—and old baths with holes—and now—prize fighters!

She goes into the kitchen, slamming the door behind her. Morgan shakes his head and goes to rejoin the group. Huw is stripped to the waist. Dai begins pinching and feeling his muscles, poking him in the ribs.

DAI (*frowning*). More in the shoulder, more in the forearm, and his legs want two more pairs like them before they will be enough.

IANTO (*quickly*). Not his fault, Dai.

DAI. No, I forgot.

He shows his one tooth to Huw in a grin of apology, then pats Huw on the back. Cyfartha also pats him.

DAI. Now—hit me by here, boy.

He sticks out his chin and touches it with a stubby forefinger. Huw hesitates. Dai touches his chin again impatiently.

DAI. Go on, boy, hit to kill.

CYFARTHA (*puffing at his pipe*). A sovereign if you will have him on the floor.

Huw, bewildered, and not at all wanting to do it, nevertheless lashes out with his fist. He catches Dai solidly. Dai takes the punch without even blinking.

DAI. Hm. Uses his shoulders well, eh, Cyfartha?

CYFARTHA. I have seen worse.

He punches the air speculatively. Dai goes down on his knees, which brings him down to Huw's height, and squares off in boxing position.

DAI. Now, look you. (*Demonstrating as he speaks*) Never swing round unless you have an opening. Jab first, then hook. The straight left first, is it? Up on your toes with your right near your chin—

As he speaks, he demonstrates. Huw copies his position. They begin to spar, Cyfartha shadow-boxing in the background. Beth reappears with the beer and slams the mugs down on the table.

The scene slowly dissolves to HUW AND MERVYN PHILLIPS squaring off. Huw stands in the correct boxing position he has learned from Dai. Both are stripped to the waist. At the beginning of the fight, Mervyn has the best of it, smothering Huw under his wild swings, but Huw keeps his head—and his feet. He begins to jab Mervyn's unprotected nose with his left. Then, when Mervyn's guard goes up, he catches him with a short right in the wind. Mervyn doubles over and Huw gives him a short left and clear right hook. Mervyn goes down in a heap, with a bloody nose. Huw looks at him in wonder. Wide-eyed, he inspects the fists that have wrought this miracle. Mervyn's sister Ceinwen, a very pretty girl about Huw's age, pushes through the crowd and goes on her knees beside him.

CEINWEN (crying). Oh, Mervyn—Mervyn—

She takes her handkerchief and tries to staunch the flow of blood, then she rises to her feet and confronts Huw with blazing eyes.

CEINWEN. You've killed him! You dirty little beast, you've killed my brother!

She goes for him fiercely. Huw backs up, trying to fend her off, then an arm comes into view and closes on her shoulder. She stops, looks up, frightened.

JONAS' VOICE. Softly, now.

Jonas is standing, holding Ceinwen, but looking at Huw. There is a smile on his lips.

JONAS. Dear me, dear me. So our coal mining friend has been indulging his favorite passion again? (Then like a lash) Go to my desk and wait.

The scene dissolves to the INTERIOR OF THE CLASSROOM. Huw and Mervyn are standing at the master's desk. Jonas is not in sight.

MERVYN (whispering). Stuff a book down your trews or he'll have you in blood.

We see the class, watching in awe and anticipation as Jonas comes in swishing a flexible, ivory-headed cane. There are a few nervous twitters from the girls in the class. CEINWEN is seen sitting near the front. She has her handkerchief, covered with her brother's blood, in her hand, and is smiling triumphantly at Huw. HUW, as he catches Ceinwen's look, sets his lips grimly. Jonas comes up to Huw and Mervyn.

JONAS (softly to Mervyn). Will you be so good as to make a back?

Mervyn obediently bends over.

JONAS (sweetly). Thank you. (Turning to Huw) Please to bend across his back.

Huw obliges. Jonas swings the cane high in the air, then brings it down ferociously across Huw's back. Huw takes the first lash. His lips tighten a little, his eyes flicker, that is all. We hear the cane descend once more. JONAS' face is twisted with sadistic pleasure as he brings the cane down again and again.

We see the faces of the children as the sound of the blows comes over. Their faces mirror their growing fear and pity at the ferocity of the caning. Last of all, we see Ceinwen. The smile of triumph is slowly going from her face as the blows fall. Her eyes are glued to Jonas' stick, moving up and down with its rise and fall. She begins to pick at her bloody handkerchief.

JONAS brings the stick down, harder and harder. Finally, it breaks. Its ivory head bounces on the floor. Jonas steps back, breathing heavily. Huw slowly and painfully straightens. Mervyn does likewise and stands watching him respectfully.

JONAS (in a squeaky, breathless falsetto). Now, then, fight again. Was just a taste. Teach you manners.

With a motion of his hand he indicates that Huw is to resume his desk. Huw looks him in the eye and Jonas' eyes avoid his look, then Huw turns and slowly makes his way down the aisle to his desk. HUW walks with pain but keeps himself erect. The other children look at him with admiration, respect and pity. Then Huw comes to Ceinwen's desk. He stops for a moment, looking down. She is looking up at him with wide eyes. The handkerchief before her is torn and shredded into little pieces. Then he moves on to his desk, slowly, still erect, and sits down.

The scene dissolves to the EXTERIOR OF THE SCHOOL. The children are passing out through the doors on their way home. Mervyn Phillips and Ceinwen appear, the latter looking round through the crowd for Huw. They stop while she looks. She still clutches the bloody handkerchief. The last of the children pass them. Then she turns to Mervyn.

CEINWEN. Go on, you. I'll be home later.

She goes back into the school.

In the CORRIDOR, Ceinwen passes through toward the classroom. She opens the door and goes in.

In the CLASSROOM, seen from Ceinwen's point of view, Huw is sitting alone at his desk. Ceinwen goes over to him. She looks down at him with great sympathy.

CEINWEN. Are you staying here, then?

HUW. For a little—

CEINWEN. And no dinner?

HUW. No.

CEINWEN. Will I get some for you? My house is close by here.

Huw shakes his head stoically. Ceinwen watches him, with tears in her eyes.

CEINWEN (impulsively). Huw Morgan— I will kiss you!

She kisses him warmly. He winces a little as her hand comes in contact with his shoulder. She is immediately full of remorse.

CEINWEN. Did I hurt?

HUW (stoutly). No!

CEINWEN. They say you had pieces of carpet down your back.

HUW. Feel if there is carpet.

She touches his back gently. He cannot control an involuntary start.

CEINWEN (crying). There is sorry I am. No carpet.

They look at each other in embarrassment for a moment, then Ceinwen speaks softly.

CEINWEN. I've got a robin's egg. Would you like it?

HUW. I have plenty.

CEINWEN. No.

HUW. Yes. Nightingales, too.

CEINWEN. Are there nightingales with you?

HUW (boasting a little). Thousands.

CEINWEN. We used to have them here, but the new ironworks burnt all the trees. (She gives him a winning smile.) May I come and listen to the nightingales with you?

CEINWEN. May I come and listen to the nightingales with you?

HUW. Yes.

CEINWEN (excitedly). When?

HUW (rather brusquely). Next summer, girl—when they are singing again.

Ceinwen is rather taken aback by this, but after a moment she recovers her composure. She looks at Huw shyly out of the corner of her eye.

CEINWEN. Have you got a sweetheart, Huw?

Huw is startled and speechless. Making a great effort, he rises, straightens his back and picks up his lunch box.

HUW. I will go home now.

CEINWEN (horrified). Across the mountain? Let my father take you—in his trap.

HUW (rather ungraciously). No—

CEINWEN. Please, Huw.

HUW (with determination). No.

He starts away from her toward the door, leaving Ceinwen hurt and disappointed. Her lip trembles a little at his rudeness.

HUW is standing in the doorway. He looks back at Ceinwen, speaks abruptly:

84

HUW. I will bring you a nightingale's egg tomorrow.

He goes out. CEINWEN's face lights up as she stands looking after him.

The scene dissolves to the VILLAGE STREET in the early evening. Huw is dragging himself painfully up the hill. He can barely walk, but his eyes are shining with pride. As he passes the Three Bells, Ivor, Ianto, Davy, Dai Bando and Cyfartha come out.

IVOR. Well—the scholar!

He slaps Huw on the neck. Huw winces, almost faints from the blow. Ianto catches him.

DAVY. What, now?

Davy peels the shirt from Huw's back and they stare at it.

IANTO (*in a whisper*). Did you have that in school?

DAVY. He has cut you to the bone, man. Who was it?

Huw will not answer.

IANTO (*quietly*). Mr. Jonas, is it?

Still Huw will not answer. Ianto's eyes turn slowly to the others.

IANTO. We will have a word with Mr. Jonas.

They all nod grimly, but Huw turns to face them.

HUW. No! Please, Davy—Ianto—I broke the rule when I fought.

DAVY (*pointing to Huw's back*). There is no rule for *that!*

HUW (*tearfully*). But he had given me warning.

DAVY. Rubbish, boy—

Ianto puts his hand on Davy's arm.

IANTO. Wait, Davy. This is Huw's affair. He shall decide it. (*To Huw*) Say the word and we will have the bones hot from his body.

HUW. Leave him alone.

Ianto nods slowly. He looks from Huw to his brothers, then back to Huw. A smile touches his lips.

IANTO (*softly*). I think our baby brother is becoming quite a man.

He takes Huw by the arm and leads him away. The other brothers follow, leaving Dai and Cyfartha looking after them. Dai's one visible eye is gleaming murderously.

CYFARTHA (*whispering*). Well—I will go to my death!

They go right back into the bar.

The scene dissolves to the INTERIOR OF THE CLASSROOM. Huw enters and approaches his desk. He stops at Ceinwen's desk for a moment, but we do not see what he does there; then he moves on to his own desk. His classmates, his former enemies, are looking at him and smiling. It is evident that he has now won his spurs as one of them. Huw does not return their looks, but keeps his eyes on Ceinwen's desk. After a moment Ceinwen hurries in and goes to her desk. She looks down at it and a pleased smile comes to her face. A nightingale's egg rests on her desk. Ceinwen looks over at Huw, trying to catch his eye. Satisfied that she has found the egg, Huw now keeps his gaze averted from her. Jonas' ruler is seen across this picture.

Jonas moves toward the blackboard with a piece of chalk in his hand. As he begins to draw some diagrams on the blackboard, the door opens in the background. Dai Bando and Cyfartha appear. They stand quietly for a moment, watching Jonas, who does not see them. Dai is dressed in his Sunday best, with a bowler hat. He carries a light cane. Huw's mouth drops open as he sees Dai and Cyfartha. He realizes that something is going to happen. Jonas is in the foreground, Dai and Cyfartha are in the background, as Jonas begins to elucidate in his usual supercilious voice.

JONAS. Yesterday the class made some progress—a very *small* progress—in the matter of linear measurements.

As Jonas talks, Dai minces toward him with his prizefighter's walk. Jonas turns curiously at this interruption.

DAI (*affably*). Good morning, Mr.—

JONAS. Jonas.

DAI (*beaming*). Mr. Jonas. (*To Cyfartha*) We have come to the right place, then, indeed.

His manner is pleasant, but his eyes are hard as ice. Cyfartha nods.

JONAS. What can I do for you?

DAI. A man is never too old to learn, is it, Mr. Jonas?

JONAS (*puzzled*). No.

He moves forward a little and Jonas backs up a few steps.

DAI. I was at school myself once. A flyweight I was, then, and no great one for knowledge.

He taps Jonas on the chest with a large forefinger.

DAI. But today, different. I am strong for learning.

They have now reached Jonas' desk and Jonas can back up no farther. Dai shoves his still smiling face within an inch of Jonas'.

JONAS (*scared*). What is it you want?

DAI. Knowledge. How would you go about measuring a stick—Mr. Jonas?

JONAS (*quavering*). By its length, of course.

DAI. And how would you take the measure of a man who would use a stick on a boy one-third his size?

Jonas gulps, with dry throat.

DAI (*conversationally*). Now you are a good man with a stick, but boxing is my subject, according to the rules laid down by the good Marquess of Queensberry.

CYFARTHA (*interjecting*). God rest his soul.

DAI. Happy I am to pass my knowledge on to you, is it? Good. From the beginning, then.

He removes his coat and bowler and hands them to Cyfartha, who brushes off the bowler and neatly folds the coat over his arm.

DAI. No man can call himself a boxer unless he has a good straight left—

JONAS (*yelling*). Help—help—

Dai drives a series of pistonlike jabs into his face.

DAI. Not to hurt your man, see? (*Jabbing*) This doesn't hurt. But to keep him off balance—

JONAS. Help! Police—

He manages to deflect one of Dai's jabs with his arm.

DAI (*approvingly*). Good—pretty blocking, there, indeed—but you left yourself open for a right hook.

He illustrates with a stinging hook to Jonas' ear. He would fall, but Dai's grip on his collar keeps him standing.

DAI. You should be able to hook with either hand—for the hook is how you will punish your man—

He illustrates with left and right hooks.

DAI. Shoulder into it—turn your fist as you hit—like that—that—that—

Jonas cries out feebly.

DAI. Keep your guard up, man! Under your chin like this. But watch your man doesn't give you a straight right in the solar plexus—

He pumps one into Jonas' ribs. Jonas' breath goes out with an "oof." His head comes down.

DAI (*going on smoothly*). —bringing your head down to where he will give you the uppercut—

He snaps Jonas' head up with a left uppercut. Jonas, his face a mess, is now moaning inarticulately, sagging in Dai's grip.

DAI. This— (*backhanding Jonas across the nose*) is against the rules—so never use it. Breaks a man's nose.

He surveys his handiwork. Jonas, moaning, suddenly goes limp. Dai shakes him and sighs as he realizes Jonas is out on his feet. He looks at the frightened class.

DAI. Eh, dear—I am afraid he will never be one to learn, eh, Cyfartha?

Cyfartha gloomily shakes his head. Dai picks Jonas up by the collar and the seat of the pants and drops him in the coal box near the stove, slamming the lid on him. As he does so, the door bursts open. Motshill, the Head, and Tyser, a junior master, rush in.

MOTSHILL (*furiously*). You cowardly brute! I will have you in court.

Dai unconcernedly takes his coat from Cyfartha and puts it on.

DAI. What for? Only a lesson it was. (*Settling his bowler*) And now home for a pint, is it? Dusty old place you have got here.

CYFARTHA. Dusty, indeed. A pint would be a blessing of good.

DAI (*tipping his bowler politely*). Good day to you, sir.

Cyfartha also tips his bowler. They go out of the room. Motshill looks after them. Jonas, a sobbing, bloody, coal-smeared wreck, crawls out of the box.

MOTSHILL (*through tight lips*). Mr. Tyser—be good enough to take Mr. Jonas home.

Tyser takes Jonas out. Motshill faces the pupils, who are all standing.

MOTSHILL. Sit down.

All sit except Huw, who remains standing, white-faced, ready to take his blame.

MOTSHILL (*sternly*). Sit down, Morgan. Huw takes his seat.

Although Motshill's face is still stern, there is the flicker of a hidden smile on his lips. He picks up a book.

MOTSHILL. Now—then—take your "Caesar's Commentaries"—

The scene fades out.

PART SEVEN

The INTERIOR OF A TAILOR SHOP, in daylight, fades in. Huw, attired in his underclothes, is standing being measured by Hwfa, the tailor, and Old Twm, his assistant. Morgan stands watching as Hwfa rolls up his tape with a snap and looks at Morgan.

HWFA. The coat will be perfect. The trews, then. Long trews or short, Mr. Morgan? Shall he be a man or stay a boy?

Huw looks at his father longingly; more than his soul he wants long trews. Morgan strokes his chin, pretending indecision. Then he smiles.

MORGAN. Long trews, of course.

Huw swells with pride. Hwfa briskly begins to assemble his tape measure, pins, etc. Huw climbs quickly into his coat and trousers.

HWFA. Good. Long it is. Come back Wednesday at half past four, and have it hot off the goose.

TWM (*with sarcasm*). And Nan Mardy coming in at the same hour Wednesday for a rain-cloak with black braid and pockets both sides.

HWFA (*angrily*). What about Nan Mardy, then?

TWM (*elaborately casual*). Only saying I was, in case.

HWFA. In case what?

TWM (*suddenly angry*). In case he has his trews about his boot tops and his shirttails above his chin, man!

HWFA. Devil fly off with Nan Mardy. A good look at a shirttail would put life in her.

MORGAN (*breaking in sternly*). Mind your tongue before the boy!

Huw, now finished dressing, is bursting with curiosity. Morgan takes his arm.

MORGAN. Come, Huw. (*To Hwfa*) He'll be here at half past four.

They go out.

OUTSIDE THE TAILOR SHOP. Morgan and Huw come out of the shop.

HUW. Why would it do Nan Mardy good to see a shirttail?

MORGAN. Mind your own business, and Nan will mind hers, and we'll all be better off.

The scene dissolves to GRUFFYDD'S ROOM. Gruffydd and Huw are working at the lathe, repairing Huw's pencil box. Huw is watching Gruffydd under his eyebrows, trying to summon up courage to ask the great question. He absent-mindedly blows some sawdust on Gruffydd, who frowns but is really amused. Huw shows what he has done to Gruffydd.

GRUFFYDD. Good. Now a piece—cross-grained—for the corner there.

But Huw doesn't move.

HUW. Mr. Gruffydd—

GRUFFYDD. Yes—

HUW. Why would it do Nan Mardy good to have a look at a shirttail?

Gruffydd, startled, looks at him.

GRUFFYDD. Where did you hear that?

HUW. From Hwfa, the tailor.

GRUFFYDD (sternly). It is a low joke, Huw. I'm surprised at you.

HUW. Is it a joke, then? Dada didn't laugh.

Gruffydd relents as he realizes the boy is in earnest.

GRUFFYDD. It means she is an elderly woman, Huw, with no husband—therefore no children. It means she would be better off with a husband.

HUW. Must she have a husband to have children?

Again Gruffydd looks startled. Huw looks at him, earnestly unconscious of any humor in his remark.

GRUFFYDD. Yes—of course. Bronwen will be having her baby any day now. She has a husband, hasn't she?

HUW (puzzled). Yes—Ivor.

GRUFFYDD. And your mother had a husband—your father.

HUW. But why?

Gruffydd studies Huw, looks him up and down, debating whether or not the time has come for Huw to learn something of "the facts of life." Huw senses that something momentous is in the offing.

HUW (hopefully). I'm getting long trews.

Gruffydd makes a big decision, then smiles.

GRUFFYDD. Very well, Huw. Then, first things first: there are some things you will know now and some things you shall wait to know. But I will give you this to think about: there are men and women. But before that, they shall be boys and girls, and before that, babies, is it?

HUW. Yes, sir.

GRUFFYDD. And before that, what?

HUW (puzzled). Nothing, sir—

GRUFFYDD. Nothing!

HUW. —like in the beginning was the Word.

GRUFFYDD (nodding). The Word was with God. And then?

HUW. Then came Adam and Eve.

GRUFFYDD. Good—. So now there was Adam and Eve in the garden and what happened?

HUW. They sinned against the Tree of Knowledge—

GRUFFYDD. Yes. What then?

HUW (not too sure of himself). Then came an Angel with a flaming sword and sent them from the Garden.

GRUFFYDD (nodding). To earn by the sweat of their brows. And what after?

HUW (this he knows). Then came Cain and Abel, and Abel was a good man but Cain killed him.

GRUFFYDD (laughs). Wait. Before to kill them, have them first. Adam and Eve we have got. Where did we have Cain and Abel?

88

HUW. From the Bible, sir.

GRUFFYDD (*a little impatiently*). But where from—to get into the Bible, boy?

There is a slight pause while Huw thinks. Gruffydd prompts him.

GRUFFYDD. Adam was created in the image of God, and Eve from the rib of Adam. But where did Cain and Abel come from?

HUW. They were the sons of Adam and Eve.

GRUFFYDD. Good! Now, what makes a man a father, and why is a woman a mother?

HUW (*deadly serious*). Well, sir, one is with moustache and trews, and the other with smoothness and skirts.

GRUFFYDD (*patiently*). No, Huw. One is a husband and the other is a wife. As Eve was the wife of Adam, and they were the father and mother of Cain and Abel, so a child must have a father and a mother and they must be husband and wife. As there is a time for everything, marriage is the time for having children so—some day—as you will be a man— you will also be a father and the girl you marry will be a mother. Like Ivor and Bronwen today.

Huw nods, dimly comprehending. Gruffydd spins the lathe.

GRUFFYDD. And there you are.

HUW. Is that all, sir?

GRUFFYDD. Is that all? What more then?

HUW. I thought it was something terrible.

Gruffydd's manner changes. His face grows very grave.

GRUFFYDD. It is terrible, Huw. Indeed terrible. Think, Huw—

He rises from the lathe. He is thinking now, not of Huw, but of Angharad and the children he will never have. He moves a few steps away from Huw, leaving Huw, wide-eyed, in the background.

GRUFFYDD (*in a low voice*). To ask the woman you love to share not only your home, your wealth— (*The thought of Angharad grows stronger.*) —your poverty— (*He pauses for a long moment, drawing a deep breath.*) —but to share the responsibility of creating life in the image of your God. Many lives, perhaps. Think of the miseries and afflictions that can come to those lives beyond the span of your own. Think to have small children in your own likeness standing at your knee, and to know them as flesh of your flesh, blood of your blood, looking to you for guidance as you look to God the Father for yours. Can that be anything but terrible, in majesty and in beauty beyond words?

Huw stands impressed but bewildered.

HUW. But why would it do Nan Mardy good to see a shirttail?

Gruffydd turns, looks at him sternly.

GRUFFYDD. I told you that was a low joke and not worth repeating. Home to your supper, now.

Before Huw can move, the sound of the mine whistle comes over, blowing in a series of short staccato blasts. Gruffydd and Huw exchange a look and run out of the house. In the VILLAGE STREET men and women are running up toward the mine. The whistle blows discordantly, shouting: "Accident." Gruffydd and Huw join the others hurrying toward the mine.

OUTSIDE THE COLLIERY the great winding wheel is slowing to a stop. The cage is coming to the surface carrying a group of miners, among them Ianto and Davy. There is a canvas-covered bundle on the floor of the cage. Ianto and Davy's faces are very grave. Gruffydd and Huw appear, hurrying toward the cage. They meet Ianto and Davy, sensing at once from their expressions that the tragedy concerns them.

IANTO. Ivor—

Huw's eyes widen.

DAVY. Slipped under a tram on the lower level.

They start down the hill toward Ivor's house.

In the STREET, as Ianto, Davy, Gruffydd and

Huw move toward the house, Bronwen appears, walking slowly, with an expression that shows that she has a premonition of what has happened. She clutches Ianto by the arm. He cannot find words to tell her what has happened.

BRONWEN (*breathing it*). Ivor?

Ianto and Davy nod. Bronwen stares, then her eyes close, her knees give way and she faints against Ianto, who supports her.

GRUFFYDD (*to Huw*). Fetch Dr. Richards —quickly!

Huw runs out of sight as Ianto and Davy carry Bronwen into her house.

The scene dissolves to BRONWEN'S PARLOR at night. The only sound in the room is a clock ticking on the mantelpiece. It is between two and three o'clock. Gruffydd, Morgan, Huw, Ianto and Davy are waiting, their eyes on the stairs. All look haggard from their vigil. Beth comes slowly down the stairs. Her sleeves are rolled up. She looks haggard, too, depressed, but indomitable. She walks over to Morgan, who is standing beneath the framed picture of Queen Victoria on the wall, under which hangs the baton the Queen gave Ivor.

BETH (*quietly, with a twist of her lips*). We have our first grandson, Gwil—

MORGAN (*nodding solemnly*). Give one, and take the other.

Beth's eyes blaze. Her voice shakes a little as she replies fiercely.

BETH. Go to that girl up by there and say that to her. She will have an answer for you.

MORGAN. Hisht, now, Beth. Do not kindle the wrath.

BETH. To hell with the wrath! (*As she speaks she lifts her eyes*) And I said it plain to be heard.

The scene fades out.

PART EIGHT

HUW'S GRADUATION CERTIFICATE, held in Morgan's hands, fades in. Then we are in the MORGAN PARLOR. Morgan and Beth are looking at the certificate. Bronwen is sitting in the background with her baby.

MORGAN (*studying the certificate*). Good with honors then. (*Smiles*) Our son is a scholar.

Beth takes the certificate, peering at it with wonder.

BETH. What is this, Huw? I can make no sense with it.

MORGAN (*proudly*). Latin, it is.

BETH. Latin, is it?

She puts down the certificate and takes Huw's head in her hands, looking at him with loving eyes.

BETH. My poor Huw. Have they stuffed your head with Latin, then?

She passes her hand over his head almost as if to see if the knowledge would show in great bumps.

MORGAN. Now, then. What will you do?

To Cardiff to school? The University and then to be a lawyer, is it? Or a doctor?

BRONWEN (*with a twinkle*). Dr. Huw Morgan— Well that will be something special—

BETH (*approvingly*). Yes, indeed—and a lovely horse and trap with a good black suit and a shirt with starch. Oh, there is good, my little one. (*Briskly*) Now, then. A glass of buttermilk for you and all your knowledge.

HUW (*smiling*). Yes, mother—(*with a sideways look at Bronwen*)—and some of Bron's shortcake.

Beth on her way to get the buttermilk, stops and puts her hands on her hips.

BETH. Oh—and my shortcake is to be fed to the pigs, is it?

HUW. No. Only I finished it yesterday, and today is shortcake day with Bron.

Bronwen looks over at Huw with the ghost of a smile.

BRONWEN. I'm sorry, Huw—only currant bread I made today. Nobody to eat it now.

Silence falls on the little group. Bronwen's eyes are shining with unshed tears. She rises and goes toward the door. BRONWEN is at the door, leaning her forehead against the door jamb, holding her baby.

BRONWEN. Oh, mother, I am lonely without him. I put his boots and clothes ready every night. But they are there, still, in the morning. (*Her voice catching on a sob*) There is lonely I am.

She goes out of the house.

Morgan, Beth and Huw look after Bronwen with shocked eyes. Then Beth steps into the kitchen for Huw's buttermilk. She comes back with a glass and pitcher as Morgan and Huw are still looking after Bronwen. Beth pours the buttermilk and gives it to Huw.

BETH. Gwil—I will have Bron here to live—if she will come.

MORGAN (*shaking his head*). Not Bron—one mistress in a house.

He sighs, then taps the graduation certificate on the table.

MORGAN. Now, then, Huw. What will it be?

Huw looks toward the door after Bronwen, then back to his father.

HUW. I will go down the colliery with you, sir.

MORGAN. Have sense, Huw. The colliery is no place for you. Why not a try for a respectable job?

BETH (*snorting*). Respectable. Are you and his brothers a lot of old jailbirds, then?

MORGAN. Leave it now, Beth. I want the boy to have the best.

BETH (*stubbornly*). If he is as good a man as you and his brothers, I will rest happy.

MORGAN. Beth—I am thinking of the boy's future. It was different in our time. There was good money and fair play for all. (*Tapping the graduation certificate on the table*) And Huw is a scholar. Why take brains down a coal mine?

HUW. I would rather, sir.

Morgan drops his hands with a gesture of helplessness.

MORGAN. Decide for yourself, then. And blame yourself if you are wrong.

HUW. The colliery.

MORGAN. Very well. That settles it— The colliery—

BETH. Good.

MORGAN (*bleakly*). Good. I am going to get drunk.

He turns and walks out of the room. Beth and Huw look after him.

HUW (*abruptly*). Mother—could I go down and live at Bron's?

Beth is startled at first.

BETH. Huw—

Huw understands that it is because she doesn't want to lose another of her sons.

HUW. It's only down the street, mother.

Beth considers the idea.

BETH. Yes—it is not good for her to be alone so much— (*Nods with decision*) Yes, go, Huw—until she marries again, you will do.

Huw, about to rise, stares at her. This possibility had not entered his mind.

HUW. Marry again? Bron?

BETH. Yes, boy—she is young, still. She has years of beauty yet— And no wages going into the house. Another husband, then—quick, too.

Huw thinks a moment, then rises.

HUW. I will go and see her.

He exits.

In BRONWEN'S HOUSE, in daylight, Bronwen is sitting in her rocking chair, rocking slowly back and forth. The baby is in her arms and she is gently stroking its hair. She turns with a sudden brightening of her eyes, as if she half expected Ivor to come in. Then the sadness is back on her face.

BRONWEN. Yes?

Huw comes quietly in. He crosses over to stand looking down at her.

HUW. I am going down the colliery, Bron.

A smile touches Bronwen's lips.

BRONWEN. Well—down the colliery. The old coal will be shaking in its seam.

Huw, however, is still very serious.

HUW. Bron—would you have me in the house to live?

She looks at him with widened eyes.

HUW. And have my wages?

Bronwen shakes her head gently.

BRONWEN. Your home is with your mother.

HUW. It was she who sent me.

BRONWEN. From pity.

HUW. No, from sense. If you put clothes night and morning, let them be my clothes.

BRONWEN (with a little smile). Good old man.

HUW. Yes, or no, Bron?

BRONWEN. Yes.

HUW. Good. I will get my bed.

Huw hurries out.

In the STREET, Huw runs from Bron's house to his own.

The scene dissolves to the MINE ENTRANCE. The day shift is going to work. Among the miners as they pass are Ianto and Huw, who is a breaker boy.

The scene dissolves to the MINE CAGE as it drops down the long shaft. The rough walls of the shaft appear to be moving swiftly up. Huw is prominent among the miners huddled in the cage. There are two or three other boys, slightly older, in the cage.

The scene dissolves, successively, to Ianto and Huw working through the day: Ianto monotonously swinging his pick into the coal face, Huw carrying the coal back and loading it on the tram at the foot of the cutting, piling the slag to shore up the walls as they progress into the seam.

HUW'S VOICE. —to work then, to earn bread for those one loves. To grow pale in the damp underground—to know hours, weeks, and months in the dark, with the dust of the coal settling on you with a light touch you could feel—as though the earth were putting her fingers on you, to warn you that she would have you there, underneath her, on her day of reckoning.

This dissolves to the MINE ENTRANCE, in daylight. The mine cage comes to the surface and the grimy men begin to pile out. Huw and Ianto are getting off the cage. Huw, blinking, draws a deep breath and looks around him as if to drink in the blessed sunlight. Ianto extinguishes his lamp and starts out. Huw follows.

At the PAY WINDOW, the men are lining up to get their pay. Ianto, Davy an Huw are prominent in the group. Huw looks very proud as he moves along in line in front of Ianto and Davy. Then Huw, Davy, and Ianto step up to get their pay. Huw receives his money and moves on, but Davy and Ianto stop at the window. They have received slips of paper with their money. Huw stops and turns back as he sees that something is wrong. They grimly show him their slips of paper.

HUW'S VOICE. To know the blessed relief when the whistle blew and the shift was ended. To stretch aching muscles—and when we came up into the light again, to know with thanksgiving, why we mining people sit out on our doorsteps when the sun is shining.

But I felt a man now in truth, to be coming up among that crowd of men, sharing their tiredness, blacked by the same dust—greeting the light with the same blinking in my eyes, thinking with *the same mind, of them, with them, a part of them. Among men, a man.*

But with my happiness came sorrow. Ianto and Davy, the best workers in the colliery, but too highly paid to compete with poorer, more desperate men.

The scene dissolves to the EXTERIOR OF THE MORGAN HOUSE, in daylight. Ianto and Davy, carrying bundles and wearing their caps, come slowly out of the house. Morgan, Beth, Bronwen and Huw stand in the door looking sadly after them. They come down the path, wave once and trudge away up the street. We follow them until they are out of sight over the hill.

HUW'S VOICE. *In my family now only two to earn wages. My father—and myself.*

The scene dissolves to the MORGAN PARLOR at night. HUW'S ATLAS stands out. The book is opened at a Mercator's Projection of the World. Huw is ruling lines from Wales to America, New Zealand, Canada and Cape Town. Now Beth and Morgan are seen looking over Huw's shoulder.

BETH. What is this old spider, now then?

HUW (*smiling*). One line from us to Owen and Gwil. (*He traces the lines with his fingers as he speaks.*) Down to Cape Town to Angharad. Over here to Ianto—in Canada—here to Davy—in New Zealand—

Huw smiles up at his mother, and puts his finger on the point from which the lines radiate.

HUW. And you are the star, shining on them from this house all the way across continents and oceans.

BETH (*with irony*). All the way? (*A little bitterly*) How far am I shining, then, if you can put it all on a little piece of paper?

MORGAN. A map it is, Beth, my little one —a picture of the world, to show you where they are.

BETH (*grimly*). I know where they are without any old pictures and spiders with a pencil!

She turns to leave them at the table and goes slowly away. She stops, turns and looks back at them.

BETH (*flatly*). They are in the house.

She turns and goes.

Huw and Morgan are looking after her as she goes into the kitchen. The scene fades out.

PART NINE

The EXTERIOR OF BRONWEN'S HOUSE fades in. Huw, grimy and in his working clothes, in a crowd of other miners, comes hurrying down from the colliery and into the house.

The INTERIOR OF BRONWEN'S HOUSE as Huw comes in. He stops suddenly as he sees Matt Harries, a pleasant, raw-boned, not too bright young man, standing in the parlor. He is dressed obviously in his best clothes, which do not fit him very well. There is a rather pathetic bouquet of flowers on the table beside him. He is the picture of a proud and somewhat embarrassed swain. Huw looks at him without enthusiasm.

HUW. Oh—(*then grudgingly*)—Hello—

Matt beams and holds out his hand.

MATT. Hello, Huw.

Huw shakes hands rather unwillingly, looking at Matt with an unwinking and distrustful stare. Matt senses Huw's hostility.

MATT. Calling on Bron, I am, but glad to see you, too.

Huw looks past him at the flowers he has brought, and frowns in disapproval. Bronwen's voice comes from upstairs.

BRONWEN'S VOICE. Is that you, Huw?

HUW (*turning*). Yes.

He goes to the foot of the stairs and up a couple of steps. Bronwen is standing at the railing above and Huw at the foot of the stairs.

BRONWEN. I'm dressing the baby. Will you give Mr. Harries a cup of tea?

HUW (*disapprovingly*). Is he staying for tea?

BRONWEN. Yes.

She goes back to her room. Huw goes back to Harries.

Matt, his back to Huw, is just taking down Ivor's ceremonial baton, given him by the Queen, from below the signed portrait of Queen Victoria, where it hangs over the mantel. He is examining it curiously. Huw takes it from him.

HUW (*looking at the baton in his hands*). The Queen gave it to Ivor when he had the choir to sing for her.

MATT. He was a good man, Ivor.

Huw looks up at him.

HUW. Yes—

He turns the baton in his hands, looking sideways at Matt.

HUW (*in a low voice*). Matt—

MATT. Yes, boy—

HUW. There is something I ought to tell you—

MATT. Yes?

Huw hesitates as if on the point of speaking, then shakes his head.

HUW. No—not my business—

He starts to move away. Matt, following him, catches his arm.

MATT. But what is it, boy?

HUW. Let Bron tell you—

MATT. It is about— (*He stumbles.*) Bronwen—and me—?

HUW (*in a low voice*). Yes—and Ivor—

MATT (*puzzled*). Ivor?

HUW. Bron will never forget him.

MATT (*puzzled*). Of course not—

HUW (*steadily*). And she will never marry another.

Matt is stunned by this.

MATT. Has she told you that, boy?

HUW. Many times.

MATT (*stunned*). But she has said nothing to me.

HUW. No—she would not want to hurt you. But she has told me that you are wasting your time here.

MATT (*whispering*). She did?

Huw is not very good at lying, but Matt's denseness makes up for the lack. Huw nods.

HUW. She told me she was sorry for you.

Matt looks very sad. He grins a sickly grin.

MATT. Well, boy—I—I'm glad you told me. I—(*he stumbles*). Well, goodbye, now.

HUW (*politely*). Won't you stay and see Bron?

But he is hoping that Matt will not.

MATT. No. (*Gulping.*) No—I will go.

Huw nods. Matt picks up his cap, looks at the flowers, and goes. Huw looks after him, with a gleam of triumph, then sobers when he hears Bronwen on the stairs. Bronwen comes down the stairs. Through the door, she sees Matt retreating down the path.

BRONWEN. Where did Matt go?

HUW. He didn't say.

BRONWEN. But why—

HUW. He said to excuse him to you.

Since Huw turns away, a suspicion is born in Bronwen's mind.

BRONWEN. Huw—

HUW. Yes—

BRONWEN. What did you say to him?

HUW (*stalling*). To who?

BRONWEN. Matt Harries—who else?

Huw is obstinately silent. Bron shakes him lightly.

BRONWEN. What did you say, Huw?

HUW (*unwillingly*). I told him lies that made him go.

BRONWEN (*quietly*). Go to his house and fetch him back. Tell him you are sorry.

Huw turns his back to her.

HUW. I'm not sorry—and I won't fetch him back.

BRONWEN. Huw—

Bronwen looks as if she would like to be angry, but there is something pathetic about Huw's jealousy. She cannot be more than a little stern with him.

BRONWEN. He is a good man, and would make me a good husband. Why shouldn't I marry him?

HUW. Because you don't love him.

BRONWEN. He understands that. Love isn't everything. Goodness is something. And bread is something—and a roof for our heads. I can take no more from you and your good father. Would you have my little Ivor go hungry because there is no man to provide for him?

HUW. I will be the man and provide for him.

BRONWEN. No, Huw—when you are a man, your wages will not be for me.

HUW. They will be for you as long as you will have them.

BRONWEN (*with a little smile*). There is a good old man you are. But some day you will be having a wife of your own —and the lucky one she will be—and children of your own, is it?

HUW (*looking at her steadily*). No, Bron.

BRONWEN. Yes, Huw.

She smiles and runs her hand through his hair. He continues to look at her with the same expression.

BRONWEN. Now—let us forget about Matt today and have our tea together.

She goes from the room, Huw looking after her. Unshed tears gradually gather in his eyes. They are not the tears of childhood. They are maturely sad.

HUW'S VOICE. *But Bron was wrong. Bron, whom I always loved—from the first time I saw her—until now. That day,* *though I looked with the eyes of a child, I saw into the future of a man. And what I saw then has remained true all my life—I never married.*

In this I never changed. But there was change now in my Valley. The slag spread faster and faster now, devouring everything in its path—all the things put in my Valley by man and God.

My Valley—soon to be green no longer—

The scene dissolves to a full view of the VALLEY. The slag heap is now much larger. The Valley is beginning to look as it was in the opening shots of the picture: gaunt trees half buried in the slag. The little brook, now a green-scummed slough, choked with slag. A miner's house as the slag pours in on it, crushing it.

HUW'S VOICE. *Then Angharad came back —alone. She would not come to our house, but stayed at the big Evans house at Tyn-y-coed.*

The scene dissolves to the EXTERIOR OF TYN-Y-COED by day, the Evans mansion, which is the largest house in the Valley. Huw is walking up the path to the front door. He uses the great knocker, removes his cap, straightens his tie and shoots his cuffs. The door is opened by Enid, a little country maid. A short distance behind her hovers Mrs. Nicholas, a plumply disagreeable housekeeper in funeral black.

HUW (*politely*). To see Mrs. Evans, please.

ENID. Who is it?

HUW. Huw Morgan.

Inside the HALLWAY, Mrs. Nicholas sweeps forward.

MRS. NICHOLAS. Her brother, is it?

Huw nods and comes in. The maid closes the door. Mrs. Nicholas looks Huw over superciliously.

MRS. NICHOLAS. This way, please.

Mrs. Nicholas opens the drawing room door. Angharad is standing by the window at the other end of the room. Huw goes slowly in, Mrs. Nicholas remaining by the open door.

In the DRAWING ROOM, we see Angharad. She looks older now, and is dressed simply but fashionably. The change in her over the years is more marked than in any other member of the Morgan family. She comes quickly to Huw and smiles at him.

ANGHARAD. Well, Huw.

She kisses him on the cheek. Huw is impressed to meet this grand lady who is his sister. Angharad looks over at Mrs. Nicholas.

ANGHARAD. Mrs. Nicholas, will you bring tea, please?

Mrs. Nicholas curtseys and goes out, leaving the door open. Angharad takes Huw's cap from him and puts it on the window seat.

ANGHARAD. Sit down, Huw. (*He sits. She takes his hand and smiles affectionately.*) There is grown you are—and changed.

HUW. You, too—

Angharad laughs with a trace of bitterness.

ANGHARAD. I look ill and should take care of myself. Everyone coming in the house says so. So you say it and we will be finished with it. (*With an obvious change of subject*) Now tell me the news from here. How are all the boys and girls we used to know?

HUW. The Jenkins girls are married. Maldwyn Hughes has gone to be a doctor and Rhys Howell is in a solicitor's office and sending home ten shillings a week—and—(*looking at her under his eyebrows*)—Mr. Gruffydd is still first up and last to bed.

The emotion shows in Angharad's eyes. She grasps his hand.

ANGHARAD. How is he, Huw?

HUW. Not as he was.

ANGHARAD. Is he ill?

HUW. Inside. In his eyes and voice. Like you.

Angharad slowly rises to her feet, looking down at Huw. Her face has gone white, her eyes are terrible.

ANGHARAD. Go from here.

Huw slowly rises to his feet, takes his cap, then both look across the room. Mrs. Nicholas is standing in the doorway, leading Enid, who carries a tea service. She has evidently been listening. When she sees that they notice her presence, she moves briskly forward.

MRS. NICHOLAS. Now then, Mrs. Evans. Tea, is it?

ANGHARAD. Wait, Huw.

Enid carries the service to a table. Mrs. Nicholas busies herself behind it.

ANGHARAD. Leave it, Mrs. Nicholas. I will pour.

MRS. NICHOLAS (*raising her eyebrows*). Well—*I* always did the pouring for Mr. Iestyn's poor mother.

She raps Enid on the knuckles with her keys.

MRS. NICHOLAS. Thumbs off the plates, Enid.

ANGHARAD (*coldly*). That will do. Not so handy with those keys, or I will have them from you. And I will pour.

MRS. NICHOLAS (*curtseying*). Yes, Mrs. Evans. (*With an oily smirk*) A new mistress is like new sheets, yes. Little bit stiff but washings to come.

She signals to Enid to follow her and leaves the room, closing the door after them emphatically. Huw and Angharad look after them.

HUW. Why do you have her here?

ANGHARAD. Thirty-seven years in the family—or so she tells me sixty times a day. Will you have tea, Huw?

She sighs and seats herself behind the tea service.

Huw is looking gravely down at her.

HUW. You told me to go.

Angharad is genuinely sorry for her outburst.

ANGHARAD. No—stay.

She pats the settee beside her. He comes and sits down next to her. She takes his hand.

96

ANGHARAD. Huw—I am sorry I was nasty.

HUW. It is nothing, girl.

Angharad looks at him, then turns her head away as her eyes fill with tears. She gets out her handkerchief and dabs at her eyes.

ANGHARAD Eh, dear—I am like an old baby. Oh, Huw—my little one—I tried to tell mother—but I couldn't.

Then she suddenly loses control. The tears come hard now. He puts his arm round her and she sobs on his shoulder. Huw tries to comfort her.

Next we see the KITCHEN—TYN-Y-COED, by day. Mrs. Nicholas and Enid are near the table. At the door are a country couple, a man and woman who have come by to sell eggs. A boy in the background is seen filling the coalbin. Mrs. Nicholas wears an expression of righteous indignation. As she talks, she is picking over the eggs.

MRS. NICHOLAS (virtuously). Not for me to say. Only the housekeeper, I am. Thirty-seven years in the family and living to curse the day.

COUNTRYWOMAN (somewhat bewildered). Well—there is terrible, it is, whatever it is, is it?

MRS. NICHOLAS (holding an egg to the light). It will not surprise me any day to see the old master rise up white from his grave. Only the gravestone is holding him down, I will swear—

ENID. Terrible—terrible, indeed. (Puzzled.) But what—?

Mrs. Nicholas leans to whisper to Enid.

ENID (shocked). Divorce?

The bucolic pair look terribly shocked.

COUNTRYWOMAN. What?

MRS. NICHOLAS. Saying nothing I am, but that is what is in her mind. (To the countrywoman.) I will take a dozen— but to ask a shilling is robbery. (Going on.) She is here without her husband, is it? And why? Because she is in love with this preacher—

COUNTRYWOMAN (shocked). No—

MRS. NICHOLAS. Preacher, I said—Mr. Gruffydd it is.

COUNTRYWOMAN (gasping). Mr. Gruffydd?—Can it be true?

MRS. NICHOLAS. True indeed— But you will never hear it from me.

COUNTRYWOMAN. Oh, I will say nothing, Mrs. Nicholas—

MRS. NICHOLAS (hinting strongly). Oh, no—no—unless you think it is your duty.

Then she takes out her handkerchief and begins to sniffle into it.

MRS. NICHOLAS. Poor little Master Iestyn! A drab from a coal mine fouling his home, and him thousands of miles away!

The country couple shake their heads sadly and go out. After they have gone, Enid turns to Mrs. Nicholas, puzzled.

ENID (timidly). But Mr. Gruffydd has not been near the house—

MRS. NICHOLAS (with scorn). What difference is that, girl? (Brusquely) Get on with your work.

Mrs. Nicholas's tears have vanished and we see her as she is.

The scene dissolves to the MAIN HEADING OF THE COLLIERY. Huw, his eyes blazing furiously, and bleeding from a cut on his lip, is giving a terrific beating to a bigger boy, an adolescent. Huw hits him savagely again and again, knocks him up against the wall of the heading, and then, crying, to his hands and knees. Huw is about to launch himself on his victim again when some miners run into the scene and pull him away, still struggling to get back at the boy.

The scene dissolves to the STREET by day. Huw comes slowly down the hill from the colliery, walking with head lowered and fists clenched. He passes little knots of people who stare at him, some whispering behind his back, but he will not look at them. He comes to Bronwen's house, stops with his hand on the gate and looks over to his own house. From his angle we can see that the door is shut. We then follow Huw as he goes over to his own house and up the path, and to the door. The shadow of a cloud falls over him. He looks up, then goes in.

HUW'S VOICE. *The knives that can be hidden in idle tongues. For generations Morgans had lived in the Valley—and now for the first time our name was touched with slander. As the slag had spread over my Valley, so now a blackness spread over the minds of its people. Our house looked strange to me—and then I knew why. For the first time I could remember, our front door was shut tight in the daytime. At the time it seemed important to me. But later I was to remember this day for another reason. My father—and the shadow of a cloud that fell across our door. If only I had known then—*

In the MORGAN PARLOR Huw's shoulder comes into view as he opens the door. Morgan is sitting there in his mining clothes, lacing up his boots. Beth stands near him. The sunlight from the opened door falls on Morgan as the cloud passes. Morgan rises as Huw comes in, closing the door. He looks over at Huw.

MORGAN. Well, Huw—some trouble with the Philistines, then?

Beth rushes to Huw.

BETH. Oh, Huw—what is it with you? Look at your hands.

HUW. Evan John—(*bewildered and hurt*)—he—he said things about Angharad and Mr. Gruffydd.

BETH (*to Morgan*). Even the children—

MORGAN. You were right, my son— (*To Beth*) I will be back for breakfast.

BETH. You will not go to the Chapel?

MORGAN. No—(*then steadily*)—and if they do this, I will never set foot in the Chapel again as long as I live.

He turns to go.

BETH. I will have brandy broth and the sheets warm on your bed.

Morgan replies with a ghost of his old humor.

MORGAN. There is an old beauty you are.

BETH (*whispering*). Go and scratch, boy.

Morgan goes out of the house. Beth and Huw look after him. Then Huw turns to his mother.

HUW. What is this about the Chapel, mother?

BETH (*looking away*). Tonight—after the service—a deacons' meeting—over Angharad.

HUW (*shocked*). Angharad. But she has done nothing.

BETH (*grimly*). Nothing is enough for people who have minds like cesses with them. (*With tears*) Oh, Huw, my little one, I do hope from my soul when you are grown, their tongues will be slower to hurt.

HUW. But will Angharad have to be at the meeting?

BETH. No. None of us will go. But the disgrace will not stay away.

HUW. I will go, mother.

He goes out. We see him come out of the Morgan house and start for Bronwen's.

OUTSIDE THE COLLIERY. Morgan and the other men of his shift are approaching the cage. Morgan gets in, and gives a signal to the operator out of the scene. The cage goes swiftly down.

The scene dissolves to the INTERIOR OF THE CHAPEL at night. It is jammed full. All the people are in their best clothes, looking righteous. Conspicuous among them are Parry and other deacons sitting near the front. Mrs. Nicholas sits close to them. At the back, Huw, now washed and dressed, comes quietly in and sits on a rear bench. People near him look at him.

People's heads turn as Gruffydd comes in and walks quietly up to the front. He takes his place at his lectern.

Gruffydd is looking gravely down at his congregation. He begins to speak with quiet deliberation.

GRUFFYDD. This is the last time I shall talk in this Chapel—(*with infinite sadness*)—I am leaving the Valley—with regret toward those who have helped me here, and who have let me help them.

(*His voice takes on an edge of scorn.*) But for the rest of you—those of you who have only proved that I have wasted my time among you, I have only to say this—

We see the congregation waiting. Huw looks horrified at the thought of losing his friend.

GRUFFYDD'S VOICE. There is not one among you who has had the courage to come to *me* and accuse me of wrongdoing—and yet, by any standard, if there has been a sin, I am the one who should be branded the sinner. Will anyone raise his voice here now to accuse me?

Gruffydd waits, his eyes looking his congregation up and down, then he goes on with scorn.

GRUFFYDD. No. You are cowards, too, as well as hypocrites. (*With a change of tone*) I do not blame you. The fault is mine as much as yours. The idle tongues, the poverty of mind which you have displayed mean that I have failed to reach most of you with the lesson I was given to teach. (*His glance sweeps the congregation.*) I thought when I was a young man that I would conquer the world with truth. I thought I would lead an army greater than Alexander ever dreamed of, not to conquer nations, but to liberate mankind. With truth. With the golden sound of the Word. But only a few of you heard me. Only a few understood. The rest of you put on black and sat in Chapel. (*His voice becomes scathing.*) Why do you come here? Why do you dress your hypocrisy in black and parade it before your God on Sunday? From love? No—for you have proved that your hearts are too withered to receive the love of your Divine Master. I know why you have come—I have seen it in your faces Sunday after Sunday as I have stood here before you. Fear has brought you. Horrible, superstitious fear. Fear of divine retribution—a bolt of fire from the skies.

Gruffydd's face is expressive as he goes on inexorably:

GRUFFYDD. The vengeance of the Lord. The justice of God. You have forgotten the love of Jesus. You disregard His sacrifice. Death, fear, flames, horror and black clothes.

He takes hold of the lectern with both hands. His voice shakes a little as he speaks.

GRUFFYDD. Have your meeting, then. But know that if you do this in the House of God and in the Name of God, you blaspheme against Him and His Word.

He steps down from his lectern and walks quietly down the aisle. The heads of the congregation turn to follow. Huw is seen looking after his friend with tears in his eyes. Then he rises and follows Gruffydd out. In the Chapel, people are looking at each other, whispering. A few, friends of the Morgans, get up and walk out. Parry goes up in front of the Chapel.

PARRY. Wait—there is a meeting.

Other people get up to leave. One man starts to go. His wife tries to pull him back in his seat, but he pulls away and commands her to follow him with a jerk of his head. More than half of the congregation walks out. The others, the righteous ones, sit looking after them blankly.

The scene dissolves to A CUTTING IN THE COLLIERY. Three or four men are working with picks against the coal face. A boy pushes a tram with coal through the scene. Morgan comes into the scene, stops, raises his head with an expression of alarm.

MORGAN (*sharply*). Hold your picks, there.

The men stop work at once, looking at Morgan. Morgan keeps his head cocked as if listening for something. He steps forward, still listening, pushing one of the men out of his way as he looks up at the face.

MORGAN (*quietly*). Get some props. (*Then urgently*) Quick, man.

One hurries to obey. The faces of the men are grave.

The INTERIOR OF GRUFFYDD'S LODGINGS at night: there is only one lamp lit. Gruffydd's old Gladstone bag and his tin trunk lie near the door. Gruffydd is cording the trunk. He himself is dressed for traveling. He looks up as Huw comes in. Huw's manner is solemn and dejected.

GRUFFYDD. Well, Huw, I am glad you have come.

HUW. Thank you, sir. (*Hesitating*) Is—is there anything I can do?

GRUFFYDD. There is. You can do me a great service.

He takes his gold watch from his pocket and hands it to Huw.

GRUFFYDD. This watch my father gave me when I entered the ministry. Take it, Huw. It has marked time we both loved.

Huw's eyes fill with tears.

HUW (*whispering*). No—Mr. Gruffydd.

GRUFFYDD (*sternly*). A service, I said you would be doing me.

Huw fingers the watch gently, looking down at it. Then he looks up at Gruffydd. The tears are now on his cheeks.

GRUFFYDD (*leading Huw to the door*). No need for us to shake hands. We will live in the minds of each other.

Huw stops at the door, looking tearfully up at Gruffydd.

HUW. Won't you see Angharad before you go?

Gruffydd pauses. His face clouds with pain. Then he answers gently.

GRUFFYDD. No, Huw.

HUW. She wants you—

Gruffydd studies Huw for a moment, then decides to tell him why.

GRUFFYDD. Yes. Teacher and pupil we have been—but friends always. (*Quietly*) If I should see her—I could not find the strength to leave her again. (*Pausing a moment*) Goodbye, my little one—with love—

As they look at each other, the mine whistle screams once—a short blast. For a moment it does not register on them. Then it screams again. Both look toward the colliery and hurry out into the street.

The EXTERIOR OF THE COLLIERY in the evening is seen from their point of view. The whistle is going in short alarm blasts. Peo-ple are coming out of their houses, men and women running up the hill toward the colliery. Gruffydd and Huw exchange a look, then start up the hill with the others. In the STREET, Gruffydd and Huw cross, looking up toward the colliery. They are joined by Beth, who comes out of her house. No word is spoken as they come up the street. Bronwen comes out from her house to join them.

OUTSIDE THE THREE BELLS INN: Dai Bando comes out with some others. He is older now and his years in the ring have nearly blinded him. He holds a mug of beer and is quite drunk. Cyfartha, also holding a mug, follows him.

DAI BANDO (*vaguely*). What is it now—fire—flood—what?

CYFARTHA. A cave-in, they're saying.

DAI BANDO. Well. I will put my mouth to a barrel, I will, and sleep drunk for the rest of my days.

He drinks deep and hurls his mug away.

DAI BANDO (*to Cyfartha*). Come—help me up there—

A MAN. What good if you can't see?

DAI BANDO. I can still swing a pick deeper than any—come on—

He starts out of the scene, his hand on Cyfartha's shoulder.

The crowd of villagers is gathered at the entrance of the COLLIERY. The winding wheel in the close foreground is turning slowly. THE MINE CAGE comes to the surface. Able-bodied miners begin to help off those who have been slightly injured in the collapse below. Other people run into the scene and begin to carry bodies and badly injured men from the cage. Women rush forward as the men are led and carried from the cage, anxiously searching the faces of the living and the dead. One utters a cry of joy as she embraces her husband who is only slightly injured. Another, on her knees, bursts into sobs as she finds her man is dead.

Some miners hurry into the CAGE. The manager, holding a paper, comes into the scene and waves his hand. The cage goes swiftly down. We follow the manager as he moves over, passing the dead and badly injured, checking names on the list in his hand.

Huw, Beth, Bronwen, and Gruffydd arrive at the gates of the COLLIERY ENTRANCE. They are looking anxiously for Morgan, glancing at the faces of the injured men being helped away. Beth goes from man to man, looking anxiously, fearfully for her husband. Gruffydd and Huw are pushing their way through the anxious crowd toward the cage. They come close to the manager, with his list.

GRUFFYDD. Gwilym Morgan?

MANAGER. Not yet.

At the COLLIERY GATES people are still running in from the village. A carriage pulls up, driven by a plainly dressed coachman. Angharad gets out. Her clothes are in contrast to those of the miners' wives and daughters round her, but her expression is the same, for she is one of them. She hurries toward the cage and joins Beth and Bronwen, looking quickly at their faces for a sign of hope. Beth, with her eyes glued to the cage which is coming up, grimly shakes her head. Bronwen puts her arm around Angharad.

The CAGE is rising once more. The manager, Gruffydd, and others push forward to help the men off. The miners who just went down emerge, carrying three badly injured men. All are coughing and choking, with smarting eyes.

Beth, Bronwen, and Angharad are inspecting a new batch of injured men as Gruffydd comes up with Huw. He stops short when he sees Angharad and their eyes meet for a moment. Then Gruffydd turns to Beth.

GRUFFYDD. There is no word of him. I will go down this time.

Beth nods at him bravely.

HUW (bursting out). I will go with you.

Gruffydd shakes his head and pushes him back.

GRUFFYDD. Stay with your mother, Huw.

He looks at Angharad and turns to go. Angharad looks after him with tears in her eyes, fists clenched. Then impulsively she runs after him.

AT THE CAGE, which is filling with men to go down, Gruffydd turns as Angharad comes up to him, oblivious of the people around them. Now we see only ANGHARAD AND GRUFFYDD.

ANGHARAD (her heart in her eyes). Come back.

Their eyes meet with a look which cannot be misunderstood.

GRUFFYDD. Yes.

He looks at her for a moment, then turns and enters the cage. Angharad stands looking after him.

Huw suddenly leaves his mother and runs toward the cage, jumping on it just as it starts to move down. Beth gasps at Huw's action, starts to move forward, but Angharad and Bronwen restrain her.

IN THE CAGE, as it moves down, Huw and Gruffydd are in the foreground. Gruffydd does not say anything to Huw, but puts his hand on his shoulder. A voice speaks up behind him.

DAI'S VOICE. I have been so long swilling behind the tap in the Three Bells that not a button will meet on my trews.

Huw turns and sees Dai behind him, now in mining clothes.

HUW. Dai—

DAI. Who is it?

HUW. Huw Morgan—

DAI (with a grin). Huw, is it? (Then reassuringly) We will find your father —no fear. He is the blood of my heart.

IN THE HEADING: the cage comes to a stop at the bottom. Water immediately flows over its floor, for the heading is already half-flooded. Gruffydd, Dai, Huw, and the other miners step down into the swirling water. They begin to cough, their eyes smarting with the fumes.

HUW (looking at the water). To our knees already—

GRUFFYDD. They will have the pumps started soon. Come.

A miner speaks up.

MINER. Bad air. Watch the lanterns.

The lanterns flicker even as he speaks. Gruffydd pays no attention to the warning, but forges ahead. The others, tense and silent, follow, coughing, muffling their mouths and noses with their hands. The little party, lanterns held high, coughing and choking in the fumes, moves down the heading. They come to a slight rise and move up it. The lanterns once more burn steadily.

DAI (*sniffing*). The air is better here.

Gruffydd suddenly stops short, holding his lantern high.

They are faced with a pile of shale and rubble. The roof has caved in. Dai feels for the fall with his hands.

DAI (*in a whisper*). Are they under this? (*He gropes for a pick.*) No eyes needed here. Give me a pick.

GRUFFYDD. Get some props up here.

One of the men hands Dai a pick. Dai waves the others back and begins to dig into the face of the slide with his pick. Gruffydd and one of the other miners move the slag back with help from Huw and the others. Two of them carry up props, ready to shore up the roof as Dai digs.

The scene dissolves into a long view of the VALLEY. The dawn is breaking over the mountains behind the colliery. Back at the COLLIERY, men, women and children are waiting silently, tensely. Some are asleep, propped up against the wall. Beth, Bronwen and Angharad are still waiting, sitting now. Angharad's head is in Bronwen's lap, and Bronwen is gently stroking her hair.

The scene dissolves to the INTERIOR OF THE MINE. The rescue party has made progress. Gruffydd now has the pick, using it not with Dai's strength, but strongly and accurately. He is weary and begrimed. Then Gruffydd stops, staring. We do not see what he sees but he glances back at the others.

GRUFFYDD (*quietly*). Here is one of them.

The others move into the scene, pull away some rocks and bring a body out from under the slag. Gruffydd kneels beside the body, looks searchingly for a sign of life, and shakes his head.

ONE OF THE MINERS (*looking down*). Evan Lewis he was, God rest him.

Dai takes the pick from Gruffydd.

DAI. Stand back now.

He once more attacks the fall.

The scene slowly dissolves to the EXTERIOR OF THE COLLIERY in daylight. Angharad, Beth and Bronwen are waiting as before. Angharad is sitting upright now. The mine manager and two young girls are passing food and drink. One of the girls offers some to Beth. She shakes her head, still staring toward the cages.

Back in the MINE HEADING, Dai and Gruffydd are pulling another miner from under the shale. This one is alive but very weak. Dai, Gruffydd and Huw bend closely over him.

DAI. Gwilym Morgan?

The miner makes a feeble gesture.

MINER. He was just ahead of me—

He goes unconscious. Gruffydd signals to two of the rescue squad.

GRUFFYDD. Take him up to the top.

Dai again takes his pick and attacks the fall. He is growing tired now, his breath coming in short gasps, but his energy seems redoubled. Dai's face is black with dust and is glistening with sweat, his breath coming in short gasps, his great muscles trembling as he pulls loose a boulder and sends it with a mighty heave clattering back along the heading. Then he grabs in the dark and stops short.

DAI. Huw!

Huw and Gruffydd push forward beside him. Dai holds up a grimy, sodden cap.

DAI. Is this his cap?

Huw grabs it from him, examines it and nods. Gruffydd points to the side of the heading.

GRUFFYDD. Up in a stall road.

Dai spreads his great hands helplessly.

102

DAI. Clear the main or the stall road?

Huw's face shows his tortured indecision.

GRUFFYDD. There is no way to tell—

But even as he speaks, Dai clutches his arm.

DAI. Listen—

Over the scene, faintly, comes the tap-tapping of a pick. Huw, Gruffydd, and Dai stand listening. They are looking up the stall road. Then Dai swings the pick with new strength.

DAI. Stand away, now.

Dai attacks the obstruction with great blows which make the walls shudder. One of the men speaks up nervously.

MINER. Mind the roof, Dai!

DAI (gasping). Devil take the roof. God is with us, and time, too.

Dai continues to shatter the rock, Huw and Gruffydd hurling it back as fast as Dai can pick it out. Then Dai suddenly chokes, gasps, and collapses on his hands and knees. His read rolls drunkenly. Since he is utterly spent, Gruffydd takes the pick and attacks the wall. Suddenly the wall in front of them seems to give way. The pick flies from Gruffydd's hands as its point meets thin air. They have now reached a pocket in the fall. Huw looks toward the hole in the wall, picks up the lantern and worms his way through. Gruffydd follows.

Huw and Gruffydd are crouched double as they move forward in the narrow passage, holding their lanterns ahead of them. They go forward, clearing rubble out of their way. They stop, listening. Gruffydd taps with his pick against the rock. They listen again. There is no answer. Gruffydd taps once more, then feebly there are two more answering taps. Huw and Gruffydd turn and crawl painfully toward the sound. They come to another fall. Gruffydd breaks it up with his pick. Huw clears the slag. They crawl through the hole they have made and stop.

Morgan is lying cramped in a narrow place, cut and half-covered by the fallen rock. Huw and Gruffydd crawl swiftly over to him. Morgan, held as in a vise by the pile of rock, is unable to move, except for one

hand, near which lies his pick. But his eyes turn to Huw and a faint smile touches his lips.

Huw is staring down at his father. Gruffydd, after looking down, looks quicly up at the crumbling roof above them, then tries gently to dislodge some of the rocks upon Morgan. The wall shakes ominously. There is a faint rumbling. Gruffydd stops, startled, with his hand on the rock and looks down at Morgan. Morgan cannot speak, but manages to shake his head slightly, warning Gruffydd not to move the rock.

Huw, Gruffydd and Morgan are seen as one of the other men crawls through the hole with a lantern. Huw speaks without looking at him.

HUW. Chris—bring some props, quick.

CHRIS. Have you found him?

HUW (in a sob). Yes.

Chris, wide-eyed, crawls backward out of the scene.

Huw lowers himself gently down beside his father, brushing the matted hair back from a cut on his father's forehead, cradling his head in the hollow of his forearm. Morgan smiles up at him. Faintly the voices of the choir begin to sing.

> HUW'S VOICE. *I knew if we moved one stone, the roof would fall on him, for the Earth bore down in mightiness and above the Earth, I thought of houses sitting quiet in the sun, and men roaming the streets, and children playing, and women washing the dishes, and good smells in our kitchen, all of them adding more to the burden upon him. But for all the weight that crushed him I saw in his eyes the shining smile that came from the brightness inside him, like a beacon light burning on the mountaintop of his spirit, and I was filled with bitter pride that he was my father, fighting still, and unafraid. I felt him make straight the trunk of his spine as he called on his Fathers, and then I could hear, as from far away, the Voices of the Men of the Valley singing a plain Amen—*

Morgan's head moves slightly. He raises his eyes, looking beyond Huw; then his eyes slowly close. Huw sits quiet, holding him, looking at him. The voices of the choir grow louder over the scene, singing in beauty and triumph.

The scene dissolves to the EXTERIOR OF THE COLLIERY by daylight and we see Beth, Bronwen and Angharad. The voices of the choir come over faintly. Beth raises her head as if listening, then speaks very quietly.

BETH. He came to me just now. Ivor was with him— (*Bronwen turns to look at her.*) They spoke to me and told me of the glory they had seen.

Angharad looks at her mother, then off toward the cages. Her eyes are shining, sadly, but with anticipation.

IN THE COLLIERY. The cage is coming up swiftly, Gruffydd in the foreground, his head held high, a look for Angharad in his eyes. Dai Bando and other miners, weary and dejected, are in the background. Huw is on the floor of the cage, holding his father's head in his lap, looking straight ahead. The cage nears the top, and light from above appears like a halo, first on Gruffydd, then on the heads and shoulders of the men and Huw and his father.

HUW'S VOICE. *And my mother was right. Men like my father cannot die. They are with us still—real in memory as they were real in flesh—loving and beloved forever.*

The scene dissolves to a full view of the VALLEY as it was in the beginning, beautiful in the sunset.

HUW'S VOICE. *Can I believe my friends all gone, when their voices are still a glory in my ears? No, and I will stand to say no, and no again. In blood I will say no. For they remain a living truth within my mind.*

The scene dissolves to a close view of BETH at her stove as we saw her in the first sequence, smiling back at her family at the table.

HUW'S VOICE. *Is my mother gone, she who knew the meaning of my family, and taught us all to know it with her?*

The scene dissolves to a close view of THE MORGAN BROTHERS: as we saw them in the opening sequence, stepping up to throw their wages into their mother's lap.

HUW'S VOICE. *My brothers, with their courage and their strength, who made me proud to be a man among them?*

The scene dissolves to a close view of ANGHARAD sitting on the porch at the reception following Ivor's wedding, looking off at Gruffydd. Then we see Gruffydd, singing with the rest, smiling over at Huw and Angharad.

HUW'S VOICE. *Angharad—is she gone? And Mr. Gruffydd, that one of rock and flame, who in teaching me, taught the meaning of friendship?*

The scene dissolves to BRONWEN, swinging up the hill with the double basket on her hip, as Huw saw her first.

HUW'S VOICE. *Is Bronwen gone, who proved to me that the love and strength of woman is greater than the fists and muscles and shoutings of men?*

The scene dissolves to a close view of MORGAN standing with his glasses on, calling the attention of his family to Huw's prize for penmanship. Then Morgan is seen giving money to Huw after his fight at the school.

HUW'S VOICE. *Did my father die under the coal? But, God in heaven, he is with me now, in the heat of his pride in my penmanship—in his quick understanding of my troubles—in the wisdom of the advice which I never found to be wrong or worthless.*

MORGAN AND HUW are seen coming up the hill as they did in the opening sequence. They walk up the crest of the hill, Huw struggling to keep up with his father's great strides. Morgan and Huw stand in silhouette, against the golden light that bathes their Valley, with the wind blowing through their hair.

HUW'S VOICE. *Is he dead? For if he is, then I am dead, and we are dead, and all of sense a mockery.*

How green was my Valley, then, and the Valley of them that have gone.

The voices of the choir swell in mighty crescendo.

The scene fades out.

PHILIP DUNNE was born in New York City, the son of humorist Finley Peter Dunne and Olympic golf champion Margaret Abbott. He was educated in private schools and at Harvard. In 1930 he became a screenwriter, later a producer and director. Among his 36 credits are: *The Count of Monte Cristo, The Rains Came, Stanley and Livingstone, How Green Was My Valley, The Late George Apley, The Ghost and Mrs. Muir, David and Bathsheba, Pinky,* and (as director) *Prince of Players, Ten North Frederick* and *Blue Denim.* Twice nominated for Academy Awards, he received the Writers' Guild's Laurel Award for lifetime achievement and Valentine Davies Award for public service. He is the first writer to be honored with a star on Hollywood's Walk of Fame. He is a past vice-president of the Writers' Guild and governor of the Academy of Motion Picture Arts & Sciences. During World War II, he was Chief of Motion Picture Production for the Office of War Information, Overseas Branch. He has served as trustee and president of the Verde Valley School in Sedona, Arizona, and as vice-chairman of the Democratic State Central Committee of California. In recent years, he has been a syndicated essayist in newspapers and national magazines. He has published *Mr. Dooley Remembers* (Atlantic-Little Brown, 1963) and *Take Two—A Life in Movies and Politics* (McGraw-Hill, 1980) as well as short stories in *The New Yorker.* A book of essays is in the works. He is married to the former Amanda Duff. They have three daughters: Miranda, a television reporter, Philippa, a musician, and Jessica, an artist. His hobbies, past and present, include astronomy, flying, bird-watching and playing the flute, all shared with his wife, as well as (in the past) surfing, golf, tennis and polo.